Selected recipes from

THE SATURDAY EVENING POST
FAMILY COOKBOOK

Edited by
Julie Nixon Eisenhower
Frederic A. Birmingham

Indianapolis, Indiana

One of the wonderful things about cooking is that it is creative. It is an art and will always remain so.

This is not to belittle the computerized wonders of packaged and frozen foods. But the true medium of cooking is first the marketplace where decisions are made; then the planning, for the little touches that create excitement and harmony at the table; and finally in the intuitive processes of cooking, which are not matters of measurement but of experience and imagination.

Such culinary art lurks in the kitchens of a thousand farmhouses, in the little black books tucked in the top drawers of a thousand kitchens, and even more remotely, in the recesses of the minds of countless numbers who love to cook. Many and great are the cookbooks which have been written in the past, but still there is the suspicion that the best is yet to come, if ever it could be pried from its myriad hiding places in homes where a recipe means "eat" instead of "publish."

Reflecting on these things, the editors of *The Saturday Evening Post* last year decided to announce a recipe contest and to call on the households of America for their most treasured dishes. The *Post Family Cookbook* contains over 350 of these recipes, recipes which have been passed on lovingly from generation to generation. Because the *Post* is regarded as something akin to a family friend, there was a willingness on the part of *Post* cooks to share the secrets of favorite dishes, such as "Baseball Dinner," prepared for years as a family of baseball fans progressed through Little League, to Pony, and finally to Legion baseball practice. Above all, it is the human element evoked by the recipe contest which makes this cookbook special. For example, one delightful recipe for Jim's Caesar Salad has a postscript for the prospective cook: "Be prepared to be complimented."

As practical cooks for their families, a great many of the contest entrants expressed an awareness of budget planning and the time involved in preparing their recipes. Yet, hand in hand with this very real concern for prices and practicality, the entrants seemed to take a special joy and delight in cooking. Homemade breads, cakes and pies—which often require special skills and loving hands—evoked by far the greatest number of recipes from readers.

In preparing the cookbook, our thanks go to many people, but in particular to the Purdue School of Cooking, which set their experts to work for us in testing many of the recipes.

If you and your family dine the better for having experienced our book, and touch hands—perhaps only slightly dusted with baking powder—with many others in households all over the land where food is valued as nourishment for both body and spirit, we will have achieved what we set out to do in the very beginning.

Frederic A. Birmingham
Managing Editor
The Saturday Evening Post

Julie Nixon Eisenhower
Assistant Managing Editor
The Saturday Evening Post

Book design by DesignCenter, Inc.
Indianapolis, Indiana

CONTENTS

SALADS

The Sharing of the Green

RICHARD NIXON'S AVOCADO SALAD

Mash 2 medium-sized avocados. Stir into slightly thickened lemon Jell-O base made with

1 package lemon Jell-O
3 tablespoons lemon juice
1½ cups hot water

Stir in 1 can (#2) of grapefruit sections drained, and ½ cup chopped celery. Chill and unmold. Serve with a whipped cream and mayonnaise mixture.

LADY BIRD JOHNSON'S MOLDED CRANBERRY SALAD

Part of the Johnson family tradition is this salad, served for holidays with chicken or turkey.

1 envelope unflavored
   gelatin
1¼ cups cold water
1 cup sugar
2 cups cranberries

½ cup chopped celery
½ cup chopped nuts (pecans
   are excellent)
½ teaspoon salt

Cook cranberries in 1 cup water for 20 minutes. Stir in sugar and cook 5 minutes longer. Soften gelatin in ¼ cup cold water; add to hot cranberries and stir until dissolved. Set aside to cool. When mixture begins to thicken, add chopped celery, nuts and salt. Turn into mold that has been rinsed with cold water. Chill in refrigerator until firm. Unmold on serving plate. Garnish with salad greens if desired. Makes about 6 servings.

CLARE BOOTHE LUCE'S GOLDEN DOLPHIN SALAD

I never can quite make up my mind whether I prefer a Chef's Salad or a Caesar Salad. My cook, Katherine Yokoyama, surprised me by combining the ingredients of both—with an Oriental touch of her own—cutting them up into non-lipstick-smearing bite sizes. So I named the salad The Golden Dolphin after my Honolulu house. It's not only my favorite salad, but everyone else's who eats it.

1 small head iceberg lettuce
2 small heads butter lettuce
½ head romaine
¾ bunch watercress
1 small cucumber, peeled
   and diced thinly

4 slices cooked ham, diced
3 slices Swiss cheese, diced
¼ cup fresh grated Parmesan
1 small can anchovies, in 1" slices
½ cup croutons, toasted in
   garlic butter

Cut all greens into ½" lengths. Toss the above ingredients (except the croutons) lightly with the following dressing:

1/3 cup white wine vinegar
2/3 cup olive oil
Dash Worcestershire sauce
2 garlic buds—put through press

¼ teaspoon salad herbs
Dash Ajinamoto or Accent
Salt, pepper to taste

Before serving, add toasted croutons, one well-beaten raw egg. Toss lightly.

DICK VAN DYKE'S
POOR RICHARD'S SALAD

This salad was given to Dick by a friend named Richard shortly after Dick was married. It's been a favorite and a filler ever since.

1 package beef wieners chopped into bite size	4 stalks celery
½ box Velveeta cheese	10 scallions
1 medium-sized jar gherkin pickles	1 small can, drained, peas
	1 package cooked macaroni shells

Mix together, add salad herbs, ¼ cup pickle juice and lots of mayonnaise. Serve cold. A perfect picnic salad.

LUCILLE BALL'S FAVORITE SALAD

My favorite salad is one I can make in a hurry, because that's the way I do almost everything. I call it a "Tropical Treat," although I'm sure that's probably not its real name. I think the first time I tasted it was in Hawaii, but I remembered the ingredients because everyone I have served it to since has always enjoyed it. It can also serve as a dessert if you don't want to stuff your guests.

I make it in individual salad bowls, which you may or may not chill before assembling your ingredients. They consist of thinly sliced bananas, pineapple rings, finely chopped nuts, lettuce and a dressing of mayonnaise and half-and-half. After that, it's simple. Line the bottom of the bowl with crisp lettuce leaves, lay in several pineapple rings, then a layer of sliced bananas. Prepare the dressing ahead of time by combining the half-and-half with mayonnaise and stirring into a thick, creamy mixture. Spoon the dressing over the salad, sprinkle with chopped nuts, and top it with a cherry.

I usually serve this with a menu of thinly sliced steak and scalloped potatoes. It's also good with a meat casserole.

BILLY GRAHAM'S
POPPY SEED DRESSING

Mix:

1½ cups sugar	2 teaspoons salt
2 teaspoons dry mustard	2/3 cup vinegar

Add and stir thoroughly 3 tablespoons onion juice. Slowly add, beating constantly, 2 cups Mazola oil. Continue beating until thick. Stir in 2 tablespoons poppy seeds to taste. Store in refrigerator. Makes 3 1/3 cups.

AMERICAN FRUIT BEAUTY SALAD

7 Native Fruits from Florida, Michigan, California, Hawaii and Oregon make this salad "Fit for a King"!

1 pint fresh strawberries, stems removed, cut into halves
½ cup fresh or frozen blueberries
½ cup fresh or frozen pineapple, cut into chunks
½ cup fresh or frozen black, sweet, pitted cherries
2 large bananas, peeled and sliced
1 inch thick and rolled in 3 tablespoons lime juice
2 large California oranges, peeled and cubed
½ cup white seedless grapes, cut into halves
1½ cups flake coconut

Combine all fruits in a large bowl. Toss to mix. Add 1 cup coconut and toss again. Pour into a large red glass bowl. Sprinkle with ¼ cup coconut. Set in refrigerator to chill for at least 1 hour before using. At serving time, sprinkle with remaining ¼ cup coconut. Serves 8.

Mrs. Richard Borth, *Dearborn, Michigan*

FROZEN FRUIT CHEESE SALAD

1 (3-ounce) package cream cheese
2 tablespoons cream
2 tablespoons lemon juice
1/8 teaspoon salt
1 cup crushed pineapple, drained
½ cup small marshmallows
½ cup chopped pecans
1 cup Royal Ann cherries, drained and pitted
2 bananas, sliced
1 cup white grapes, seeded
2 cups whipping cream
3/4 cup mayonnaise

Work the cheese, cream, lemon juice and salt together. Add pineapple, marshmallows, nuts, cherries, grapes and bananas. Whip the cream and work the mayonnaise into it. Fold this into the fruit mixture. Freeze about 3 hours, until firm. Serve on lettuce with cream cheese dressing. Serves 18.

Cream Cheese Dressing

Cream 2 (3-ounce) packages cream cheese with 8 tablespoons vegetable oil. Add ½ teaspoon salt, 1/8 teaspoon white pepper, 1½ teaspoons sugar, 1 tablespoon lemon juice. Dust with paprika.

Dorothy Imlay, *St. Joseph, Missouri*

AUNT IRENE'S CHERRY-PINEAPPLE SALAD

2 (3-ounce) packages cream cheese
1 cup mayonnaise
1 cup maraschino cherries
1 (#2) can pineapple chunks, drained
2½ cups small marshmallows
1 cup whipping cream

Combine cheese and mayonnaise and blend until smooth. Fold in fruit, marshmallows and cream which has been whipped. Chill. Serves 8 to 10.

Mrs. Adolph Voelker, *Tell City, Indiana*

APPLE ORCHARD SALAD

1 envelope unflavored gelatin
¼ cup sugar
1 3/4 cups cranapple juice
2 tablespoons lime juice
½ cup chopped unpeeled apple

½ cup finely chopped fresh
 cranberries
½ cup chopped celery
1 (3-ounce) package cream cheese
½ cup finely chopped walnuts

Mix gelatin and sugar in saucepan. Stir in 3/4 cup of the cranapple juice.
Place over low heat, stirring constantly, until gelatin is dissolved, about 3 to
5 minutes. Remove from heat; stir in remaining 1 cup cranapple juice and
lime juice. Chill, stirring occasionally, until slightly thicker than the consistency of unbeaten egg white. Add chopped apple, finely chopped cranberries
and celery. Cut cream cheese into 12 squares, roll into balls and then roll in
chopped walnuts. Put 2 cream-cheese balls in each of 6 individual molds,
then spoon in gelatin mixture. Chill until firm. Unmold and garnish with
lettuce. Serves 6.

Mrs. C. Mize, *High Point, North Carolina*

APRICOT ALLURE SALAD

1 small package lime Jell-O
3/4 cup sugar
1 (#2) can crushed pineapple
1 cup cranberry cocktail
1 (3-ounce) package cream cheese
1 cup dried apricots, chopped fine

1 cup whipping cream
1 cup finely diced celery
1 cup mixed chopped nuts
1 pound chocolate-covered
 maraschino cherries

Combine Jell-O, sugar and pineapple. Heat until mixture simmers. Then add
cranberry cocktail, crumbled cream cheese and finely chopped apricots. Mix
thoroughly. Remove from heat and cool until chilled. Whip cream and blend
with above mixture. Add finely chopped celery and top with nuts and chill.
When ready to serve, crush two or three chocolate-covered maraschino
cherries over top of each serving. Serve on lettuce or with other greens.
Serves 8.

Mrs. Vincent Garner, *Valencia, Pennsylvania*

LOVELY LEMALOHA SALAD

1 (6-ounce) package lemon gelatin
1 cup boiling water
2 cups ginger ale
1 (20-ounce) can crushed pineapple
 in juice
1 (8-ounce) can imitation

sour cream
1 tablespoon crème de menthe
 syrup
1 dozen pineapple chunks, well
 drained

Dissolve gelatin in boiling water. Remove ¼ cup and reserve for topping. Add
ginger ale and crushed pineapple. Pour into a 12-by-12-by-2-inch dish and
refrigerate until solid. Combine reserved gelatin, sour cream and crème de
menthe syrup in medium bowl; chill. To serve, cut pineapple gelatin into 12
pieces. Place each on a leaf of lettuce on a serving plate. Garnish with a
dollop of sour cream mixture and a pineapple chunk. Makes 12 servings.

Mrs. Marcia Mae Curtis, *Winslow, Indiana*

CABBAGE AND FRUIT SALAD

1½ cups white cabbage
½ cup red cabbage
½ cup carrots
½ cup walnuts
2 to 3 bananas, not overripe
2 to 3 apples

1 can mandarin oranges, drained
1 small can crushed pineapple, drained
1 cup miniature marshmallows
½ cup white grapes, halved

Dressing

¾ cup mayonnaise
¼ cup plain white vinegar
3 to 4 tablespoons sugar

Chop white and red cabbage, carrots and walnuts very fine. Dice bananas and apples and add to cabbage mixture. Add mandarin oranges, pineapple, marshmallows and grapes. Combine mayonnaise, vinegar and sugar; place in jar with tight lid and shake thoroughly. Pour over cabbage and fruit and mix. Garnish with maraschino cherries or orance slices. Serves 8.

M.L. Savidge, *Fair Oaks, California*

WARM CABBAGE SLAW

3 pounds cabbage
¼ cup vinegar
¼ cup water
1 teaspoon salt

¼ teaspoon caraway seeds
½ teaspoon sugar
3 rashers bacon

Wash and shred cabbage; drain. Cook vinegar, water, salt, caraway seeds and sugar. Pour over cabbage. Let stand for 15 minutes. Remove cabbage. Bring liquid to a boil again. Pour over cabbage. Do this 3 times. Fry bacon until crisp. Sprinkle over cabbage. Serves 6.

Mrs. Joe Hrvatin, *Spokane, Washington*

"Now here's a dinner fit for a King . . . Here, King!"

JIM CAESAR'S SALAD FOR SIX

2 cloves garlic, crushed
3 ounces olive oil
5 tablespoons wine vinegar
1 can flat anchovies

1 (6-ounce) can Parmesan cheese
1 lemon, cut in half
1 raw egg
2 heads fresh, crisp romaine lettuce

Place wooden salad bowl and individual salad bowls into refrigerator for several hours before preparing salad. Also place washed lettuce in refrigerator for 2 to 3 hours before use. When your guests arrive, announce to them that you are going to make a very special salad to be prepared at the table by yourself. About 15 minutes before serving, garnish entire surface of salad bowl with garlic, half the olive oil and half the vinegar. Mash half of the anchovies against the sides of the bowl. Sprinkle a little Parmesan cheese until a pasty consistency covers the entire surface. Place the bowl back in the refrigerator for 10 minutes. Seat your guests and have your wife, or butler, bring the salad bowl and six individual bowls to the table. Squeeze the lemon and add the remainder of the anchovies. The climax is breaking a raw egg into the bowl. Stir vigorously with a real connoisseur's flair. Add the crisp chilled lettuce. In a zigzag motion add the remaining oil and vinegar. Toss lightly, be careful that each piece of lettuce is coated. Sprinkle with Parmesan cheese and add croutons. Serve immediately. Be prepared to be highly complimented!

James Clifton Bates, *Chamblee, Georgia*

IDEAL COMBINATION SALAD

Red leaf and head lettuce,
  broken into bite-size pieces
1 carrot, grated
2 stalks tender celery,
  cut in small pieces

2 green onions, diced
½ tart apple, diced
½ cucumber, diced
2 firm tomatoes, wedged
1 firm banana, sliced

Dressing:

1 cup mayonnaise
2 tablespoons chili sauce
1 tablespoon wine vinegar

1 teaspoon lemon juice
1 teaspoon sugar

Mix dressing ingredients well. Toss lettuce with vegetables and fruit. Add dressing and toss together gently.

Mrs. Margerite K. Hubbs, *North Hollywood, California*

SEIDEL'S SALAD DRESSING

Juice of one lemon, or
  2 tablespoons vinegar
1 tablespoon catsup
1 tablespoon salad oil
2 teaspoons Worcestershire sauce
1 tablespoon sugar

½ teaspoon salt
¼ teaspoon paprika
1/8 teaspoon garlic powder
1/8 teaspoon black pepper
Chopped parsley

Mix all ingredients together and serve over salad greens. Yield: 4 servings.

Carl Seidel, *St. Paul, Minnesota*

AMBROSIA ORIENTAL SALAD

2 cups cooked shrimp
1 cup mandarin oranges
1 cup pineapple chunks
1 small can sliced water chestnuts
4 cups lettuce torn into
  bite-size pieces

1 cup diced celery
½ cup sliced onion
  separated into rings
¼ cup chopped green pepper
¼ cup flaked coconut
1/3 cup cashew nuts

Place lettuce in large salad bowl. Combine remaining ingredients. Place on top of lettuce. Serve with celery seed dressing.

Celery Seed Dressing

3/4 cup sugar
1/3 cup vinegar
1 teaspoon salt
1 teaspoon dry mustard

1 teaspoon grated onion
1 cup salad oil
1 tablespoon celery seed

In mixer bowl, combine first five ingredients. Mix thoroughly. Add oil slowly. Beat with electric mixer until thick. Stir in celery seed. Refrigerate until needed. Makes 1 3/4 cups. Serves 4.

Marjorie V. Anderson, *Mt. Zion, Illinois*

CHINESE CENTURY SALAD

1 (18-ounce) can bean sprouts
3 carrots
2 green peppers
½ cup fresh mushrooms, sliced thin
4 thin slices baked or boiled ham

1 red pimiento, sliced
1 cup shrimp
2 teaspoon soy sauce
1 inch fresh ginger,
  peeled and grated.

Drain bean sprouts well. Cut carrots into thin strips. Shred peppers. Wipe mushrooms, trim the stalks, and cut into thin slices. Place ingredients into a large salad bowl. Cut ham and red pimiento into thin strips and add to the bowl. Add shrimp. Mix soy sauce with fresh ginger and garlic dressing. Pour over salad and mix until well coated. Serves 4.

Garlic Dressing:

4 tablespoons salad oil
2 tablespoons apple cider
½ teaspoon white pepper

½ teaspoon dry mustard
1 clove of garlic, crushed

Combine all ingredients in a glass jar. Shake until well blended.

Pat O'Brien, *Detroit, Michigan*

SHRIMP SALAD SUPREME

1 small can tomato soup
1 (8-ounce) package cream cheese
2 packages plain gelatin,
    dissolved in ½ cup cold water
½ cup mayonnaise
½ cup stuffed olives, chopped
½ cup slivered almonds
1 cup chopped cucumber
2 cups tiny cooked shrimp

Heat soup. Gradually add cream cheese and stir until melted. Add gelatin; stir well and cool. Beat in mayonnaise, and stir in olives, almonds, cucumbers and shrimp. Chill until firm and serve on greens with favorite dressing. Serves 6.
Mrs. J. R. Hickman, *St. Petersburg, Florida*

15

TUNA SALAD NIÇOISE

2 (6½-ounce) cans tuna
4 stalks of celery
1 small onion, chopped
12 pitted black olives, sliced
    in half
4 hard-boiled eggs, sliced in half
4 large crisp lettuce leaves
4 cherry tomatoes

Drain tuna and break into small chunks. Combine first 4 ingredients in bowl. Place a lettuce leaf on each of 4 plates. Divide tuna mixture into 4 portions, placing each portion on a lettuce leaf. Top with hard-boiled egg wedges and cherry tomatoes. Pour 1 tablespoon dressing (combine 2 tablespoons lemon juice, 1 tablespoon water and 1 tablespoon vegetable oil) over each serving. Serves 4.
Louise Rotello, *Tucson, Arizona*

"Take over for a while, Joe. I'm going out for lunch."

TANTALIZING TOMATO SALAD

2 tablespoons unflavored gelatin
½ cup cold water
1 (10½-ounce) can tomato bisque
  or soup
1 (3-ounce) package cream cheese
½ cup small curd cottage cheese

1 cup mayonnaise
1/3 cup finely chopped celery
1 tablespoon finely chopped
  green pepper
½ cup sliced green olives

Soften gelatin in the ½ cup cold water. Heat soup and stir in gelatin until dissolved. In bowl, mash cream cheese; then stir in cottage cheese, mayonnaise, celery, green pepper. Add cheese mixture to soup and gelatin. Gently fold in sliced olives. Pour into individual molds (or one large mold) and chill until firm. Makes 8 servings.

Joyce Y. Schultz, *Louisville, Kentucky*

HOLIDAY TURKEY SALAD

1 small package lemon
  or lime gelatin
2 cups leftover turkey stock
3/4 cup cooked peas
3 medium-sized carrots,

grated
½ cup celery, chopped
½ cup fresh raw green pepper, grated
2½ cups cooked turkey, diced

Dissolve gelatin in hot turkey stock. Cool until slightly thickened. Combine peas, carrots, celery, pepper, turkey. Blend well by hand. Add to gelatin mixture. Pour into mold. Chill. Serves 6.

Mrs. Mary R. Asbeck, *North Little Rock, Arkansas*

TEN BEAN SALAD

1 can each, drained and rinsed:
  Garbanzo beans
  Red kidney beans
  Pinto beans
  Soy beans
  Butter beans
  Lima beans

  Green beans—cut
  Wax beans—cut
Bean sprouts
Great northern beans
1 green pepper, chopped
1 small onion, chopped

Dressing

1 cup sugar
1 cup vinegar

3/4 cup oil
Salt and pepper to taste

Mix dressing ingredients and pour over the beans, pepper and onion. Refrigerate overnight before serving. It improves with age. Serves 10 to 12.

David Savidge, *Fair Oaks, California*

VEGETABLES

Let Them Eat Spinach

MARINATED MUSHROOMS FOR A CAMP TRIP
By Roy Andries de Groot

One remembers the morning brilliance of the hills, the song of the racing stream, the last flip of the rod. The rainbow trout that flashes in the sunlight and lands on the bank will never be as perfect to eat as at this moment. Neither banquet nor restaurant can produce the delight of feasting on foods freshly gathered and eaten beneath sun or stars. Too many picnics are bogged down by an overabundance of packaged foods and household trappings which provide so little contrast from the everyday routine that one might as well have stayed at home. The basic rule for eating out of doors is that the food should be prepared and presented with natural simplicity. Prepare marinade at home. Heat in saucepan:

1 cup water
½ cup olive oil
¼ cup tarragon wine vinegar
1 teaspoon salt
12 whole peppercorns

1 teaspoon monosodium glutamate
2 whole bayleaves
1 teaspoon fennel seed
½ teaspoon thyme
4 whole sprigs parsley

Simmer 10 minutes to develop flavor, then cool and store in screw-top jar. At campsite, bring marinade to boil in a largish pan, then drup in 1 dozen or more button mushrooms and simmer about 20 minutes. Let cool in marinade, drain and serve as appetizer.

MRS. GERTRUDE CRUM'S FAVORITE RECIPE: MUSHROOM CASSEROLE

2 lbs. mushrooms
  (use caps only)

For Mushroom Béchamel:

4 tablespoons butter
4 tablespoons flour
1 cup light cream
3 eggs
  (separate whites from yolks)
Salt, white pepper

Extra butter for sautéing
  mushrooms

Chop mushrooms caps. Sauté in butter 5 minutes. Drain and reserve dark, buttery juice. Yield: about 1 cup juice and 2¼ to 2½ cups sautéed mushrooms. Make a roux of 4 tablespoons butter and 4 tablespoons flour, mushroom juice and light cream. Use half cream, half juice; i.e. 1 cup of each. Result: a thick rich béchamel of pronounced mushroom flavor. You will have 2 cups of this mushroom béchamel. You will need only 1 cup for the mushroom casserole. Save the remainder for a heavenly mushroom soup. Cool the béchamel and add 1 cup to sautéed mushrooms. Beat yolks of 3 eggs and add to sautéed mushroom-béchamel mixture. Add salt and pepper to taste. Remember that adding the whites will reduce flavor. Beat the egg whites until they are stiff and fold them into the first mixture. Bake in buttered casserole or soufflé dish in moderate 350° oven in pan of water 40 minutes or until set. Serves eight. Note: this is such a marvelous dish it deserves a party.

AUNT ROSE'S
CAPE COD BAKED BEANS

1½ pounds yellow eye beans
¾ pound salt pork, sliced
1 large white onion, thinly sliced

1 pound fresh spareribs, cut into
separate ribs

Soak beans overnight. In morning, boil in same water with pinch of baking soda for 15 minutes. Drain beans and rinse in cool water. Put layer of beans in bottom of bean pot, then layer of salt pork strips and onions. Then more beans followed by a layer of spareribs. Repeat layers. The top layer should be a strip of salt pork.

Topping:

Generous ½ cup of dark molasses
Heaping tablespoon brown sugar
1 teaspoon dry mustard

Pinch cayenne pepper
Boiling water to fill pot

Bake at 275° for 6 hours. During last hour, add 1 teaspoon salt and 1 tablespoon butter. Remove lid of bean pot for last 15 minutes. This recipe is older than Boston baked beans. Serves 6.

Joan Nickerson, *Brewster, Massachusetts*

PICKLED BEET AND EGG NEST

Pickled beets and eggs in a uniquely flavored beet juice gelatin. Nest-shaped in a 3-cup ring mold. At serving time, fill "nest" with shredded lettuce, chilled olives (black and green), radishes, cucumber slices and small celery pieces.

1 package unflavored gelatin
1 (16-ounce) can sliced beets
¾ cup beet juice (use
   juice from beets,
   if not enough to measure
   ¾ cup, add water)

¼ cup wine vinegar
¾ cup cold water
1 tablespoon sugar
1 tablespoon (heaping) mayonnaise
1/8 teaspoon Worcestershire sauce
2 hard-cooked eggs, sliced

Pour half of the beet juice over unflavored gelatin to soften. Place on low heat to melt. Add remaining beet juice, vinegar and cold water. Chill until the consistency of egg white. Combine sugar, mayonnaise and Worcestershire sauce; blend, and add to chilled beet juice; add beets and eggs and mix well. Turn into 3-cup ring mold; chill until firm. Unmold on serving plate garnished with salad greens and fill nest with olives, radishes, cucumber slices and celery pieces. Serves 4 to 6.

Mrs. Harold Johnston, *Anaheim, California*

19

BROCCOLI AT ITS BEST

2 (10-ounce) packages
  frozen broccoli
1 cup Velveeta cheese (cut into
  ½-inch cubes)

1 tablespoon butter
½ cup milk
1 teaspoon nutmeg
3 tablespoons bread crumbs

Cook broccoli; drain well. Mix broccoli with the remaining ingredients and place entire mixture in a 1½-quart baking dish. Bake at 350° for 20 minutes. Serves 4.

Mrs. Rita Baur, *Arvada, Colorado*

VEGETABLE CASSEROLE

1 bunch fresh broccoli or
  2 packages frozen spears
1 (10-ounce) package frozen peas
1/8 pound butter or margarine
1 tablespoon flour
1 teaspoon salt

¾ cup milk
1 egg yolk, beaten
4 ounces process cheese spread
12 soda crackers or other salted
  snack crackers

Cook broccoli and peas very lightly. (They should still be bright green.) Prepare sauce: In medium saucepan, melt butter. Stir in flour and salt. Cook until mixture has thickened, gradually adding milk and beaten egg yolk. Cut cheese in small pieces and stir into sauce until smooth. Grease 2-quart casserole with butter. Alternate layers of vegetables and sauce, ending with sauce. Sprinkle crushed crackers on top. Drizzle with 1 tablespoon melted butter. Bake 30 minutes in 325° oven. Serve immediately. Serves 6 to 8.

Sandra Moore, *Elmhurst, Illinois*

SANDWICH ISLES CABBAGE

2 tablespoons olive oil
2 tablespoons soy sauce
1 head finely shredded cabbage
1 shredded lemon rind
1 (12-ounce) jar of chutney

¼ cup water
¼ teaspoon curry powder
½ teaspoon fresh lemon juice
1 teaspoon granulated sugar
¼ cup pineapple juice

Preheat iron skillet or Chinese wok, add olive oil and soy sauce. Add cabbage and lemon rind; stir briskly for 10 minutes on low heat. Add chutney. Mix separately the water, curry powder, lemon juice, sugar and pineapple juice. Pour contents into skillet and stir slowly for 10 minutes over low heat. Cover skillet, turn off heat and let stand an additional 10 minutes. Serve with shredded coconut. Serves 4 to 6.

Oliver Beadling, *Honolulu, Hawaii*

CREAMED CARROTS AND APPLES

2 large apples, pared and sliced
1 tablespoon sugar
2 cups sliced carrots
1 cup sour cream
Allspice

Cook the apples in two cups of water with one tablespoon of sugar. When cooked, drain and mash. Keep warm. At the same time, cook two cups of sliced carrots in salted water. Drain and mash. Combine apples and carrots. Add 1 cup of sour cream. Sprinkle the casserole with allspice. Serves 6.

Mrs. Paula Robie, *Spokane, Washington*

CHARISMATIC CARROTS

1 pound carrots
½ cup sweet white wine
(such as Sauterne or Catawba)
½ cup water

Peel carrots and cut into halves crosswise, then into quarters lengthwise. Place carrot pieces in a 6-cup deep casserole or baking dish, and pour over them the wine and water. Cover casserole tightly with foil and bake at 375° for approximately 30 minutes. Serves 4.

Georgia M. Dotson, *Washington, D.C.*

CARROTS A LA MONTE CARLO

6 whole, fresh, large carrots, peeled and sliced
½ cup thinly sliced pascal celery, including green tops, chopped fine
¼ cup water chestnuts, sliced
½ cup flake coconut
1 tablespoon capers
2 tablespoons pistachio nuts
1 cup commercial sour cream
1 teaspoon ginger
1 tablespoon Worcestershire sauce

Topping:

2 tablespoons wheat germ
1/3 cup flour
½ cup grated American cheese
1/3 cup sesame seed
2 tablespoons soft butter

Blend topping in order given with pastry blender. Use as directed. Cook carrots and celery in small amount of water until fork tender. Drain. Combine ingredients in order given. Mix well. Pour into buttered 2-quart baking dish. Bake at 350° for 30 minutes. Remove from oven. Sprinkle with topping. Return to oven at 325° for 15 minutes or until light golden brown. Serves 6.

Ann Borth, *Dearborn, Michigan*

CARROT-PARSNIP CASSEROLE WITH ORANGE-GINGER GLAZE

3 to 4 medium-size parsnips
3 to 4 sliced carrots
Orange-ginger Glaze
1 teaspoon cornstarch
2 tablespoons brown sugar
2 tablespoons butter
¼ cup orange juice

1 tablespoon pure rum extract
1 teaspoon pure orange extract
2 tablespoons freshly grated
  orange rind
1 tablespoon candied ginger
  (cut in fine slivers)
2 tablespoons orange marmalade

Wash and boil parsnips until just tender; drain. Peel and cut in ¼-inch slices. Peel and steam carrots until just done. If cores of parsnips are woody, remove them and then slice. Brown slices of parsnips in only a little butter until a delicate golden brown.

To make glaze, mix cornstarch and brown sugar. Add butter, orange juice, rum extract, orange extract, orange rind, ginger, orange marmalade. Cook until thick, stirring constantly.

Butter a flat casserole and arrange carrots and parsnips to cover the bottom. Cover with glaze and repeat layers until vegetables are used up. Dot with butter. Place casserole in pan of hot water and bake, covered, at 350° or less for one hour or until glaze has permeated the vegetables. Serve hot.

The glaze is excellent for fowl or ham, or for filling pear halves before baking. Serves 4.

Ruth G. Gleason, *Helena, Montana*

CELERY CELESTIAL

5 cups celery, cut into 1-inch pieces
1 cup carrots, sliced
½ teaspoon seasoned salt
1 cup grated cheddar cheese

2 tablespoons butter or margarine
½ can cream of chicken soup
Sliced almonds

Cook celery and carrots for 10 minutes. Drain well. Place half of the celery and carrots in a 2-quart casserole. Sprinkle with seasoned salt. Top with half of the cheese and butter or margarine. Repeat layers. Pour soup over all. Top with almonds. Bake at 350° for 30 minutes. Serves 4 to 6.

Mrs. Helene Levin, *San Jose, California*

CASHEW NUT ORIENTAL

2 cups raw cashew nuts
5 eggs
3 tablespoons oil
1 tablespoon Loma Linda Savorex
3 tablespoons dried (or fresh)
  parsley
1 cup milk

1 teaspoon sage
1 teaspoon salt
2 large onions, chopped fine
1 cup sourdough bread crumbs
2/3 cup celery, chopped
2 cups cooked rice

Combine first eight ingredients in blender until nuts are chopped medium to fine. Add onions, bread crumbs, celery and rice; pour into oiled 3-quart casserole. Set in a pan of hot water while baking. Bake in a 350° oven for 1 to 1¼ hours until casserole is hot. Serve with mushroom gravy. Serves 10.

Marian Lundquist, *San Diego, California*

CARROT-NUT STUFFED ZUCCHINI

8 zucchini
3 tablespoons lemon juice
¼ cup oil
1 teaspoon salt

1 bay leaf
1 tablespoon parsley, minced
¼ teaspoon pepper
16 teaspoons grated Parmesan cheese

Carrot-nut filling:

4 tablespoons butter
½ cup onion, chopped
3 cups grated fresh carrots
½ cup water chestnuts, chopped
¾ cup dairy sour cream

½ teaspoon nutmeg
½ teaspoon dried dill
1 teaspoon salt
½ teaspoon pepper
1 cup chopped walnuts

23

Wash, do not peel, zucchini. Cut in half lengthwise, hollow out seeds with melon ball cutter, leaving a cavity. Place lemon juice, oil, salt, bay leaf, parsley and pepper in large kettle. Add zucchini and boiling water to cover. Bring to a boil and parboil for 2 minutes. Remove; drain on paper towel, cut side down.

To make carrot-nut filling, sauté onion, carrots and chestnuts in butter until onion is golden. Add sour cream, nutmeg, dill, salt, pepper and walnuts. Heat thoroughly; do not boil. Blend well; remove from heat and fill prepared zucchini halves. When filled, sprinkle each with 1 teaspoon grated Parmesan cheese. Bake in 400° oven for 15 to 18 minutes. Serves 16.

Mrs. Albert Van Buren, *Willmar, Minnesota*

CHEESE-STUFFED ZUCCHINI

6 (8-inch) zucchini
1 cup minced onion
½ cup butter
¼ cup milk or cream
¼ cup fine bread crumbs, toasted

2 tablespoons freshly grated
  Parmesan cheese
Geoduck king clam,
  minced (optional)
Parsley

Clean zucchini well and trim stem ends. Slice off 1/3 of top of zucchini lengthwise. Blanch both sections in boiling salted water to cover for 10 minutes. Drain and refresh under running cold water. Scoop out pulp from top and bottom sections with small spoon, being careful not to tear bottom shells. Invert bottom shells on paper towels and discard top shells. Mince the pulp, squeezing out as much moisture as possible. Using large skillet, sauté onion in butter until soft, but not browned. Add minced zucchini and simmer for 5 minutes. Remove from heat and add milk or cream, bread crumbs, Parmesan cheese and geoduck (if desired). Salt and pepper to taste. Dry insides of shells with paper towels. Spoon mixture into shells. Sprinkle tops with more Parmesan cheese or geoduck, and a little melted butter. Place zucchini in a lightly buttered baking dish. Bake in preheated oven (450°) for 10 to 15 minutes or until tops are golden. Put zucchini in serving tray, sprinkle with chopped parsley and garnish with lemon wedges. Serves 6 to 12.

Veronica Mar Dolan, *Portland, Oregon*

STUFFED SQUASH SUPREME

2 large acorn squash
1 teaspoon salt
¼ teaspoon pepper
½ cup chopped celery
½ cup diced green pepper
½ cup drained mushrooms,

bits and pieces
1 teaspoon minced onion or
  ½ teaspoon onion juice
1 tablespoon chopped parsley
1 cup sour cream
¼ teaspoon allspice

Cut squash in half, remove seeds, and steam or bake until tender, about 1 hour in 350° oven. Remove pulp and mash. Keep shells. Add salt and pepper to mashed squash. Combine chopped celery, green pepper and mushrooms. Add onion and parsley. Steam vegetables until partially cooked; add to mashed squash. Fold in sour cream and fill shells. Sprinkle with allspice. Bake in 400° oven for 15 to 20 minutes. Serves 4.

Mrs. Joe Hrvatin, *Spokane, Washington*

I REMEMBER MAMA'S TURNIPS

1½ cups cooked unseasoned
  mashed turnips
3 cups hot mashed white potatoes

Salt and pepper to taste
6 tablespoons butter
2/3 cup grated process cheese

Mix turnips, potatoes, salt and pepper, melted butter. Just before serving, fold in the grated cheese. Serves 4.

Diane Ann Haley, *Clearwater, Florida*

"This place has a real homey atmosphere."

24

RICE & POTATOES

True Grits

GRITS
By Starkey Flythe, Jr.

Which brings us to grits. Much maligned—deservedly so—its main fault is the time and place of its appearance. Breakfast. They tell a story in south Georgia about a Northern salesman who very politely balked at the custom of serving grits—unasked—at breakfast. He was assured it wasn't extra and he resisted saying he didn't care for it and the waitress persisted, morning after morning, and finally he said, "I don't mind but I do hate to waste good food—why is it when I've told you and told you and told you I didn't want it you still bring it?" And she leaned forward and looked him in the eye and said, "Mister, I think it's the law."

It ought to be broken. Have it at supper. Late supper. Before the fire. Kids in bed. Just the two of you. A plate of yellow grits—that singular plural—the legendary Smithfield ham, and something dark green, spinach, collards, for a beautiful Italian tri-color. A sip of bourbon with a lot of ice taken almost like a strong wine. Ah. Double ah. That ought to be the law.

½ cups grits
1½ cups boiling salted water

Add grits slowly to boiling water and cook 30 to 40 minutes, stirring constantly.

RICE

Rice has been grown in the South since Colonial times, first in the Carolinas and now predominantly in Arkansas. Lighter than bread or potatoes, it provides a satisfying starch, low in calories and capable of astonishing variety.

Parsleyed rice provides a green vegetable as a rider with none of the fuss or it's-spinach-and-I-won't-eat-it-attitude most children have about green things. Simply add a cup of fresh parsley to 1 cup of boiled rice. Keep a pair of scissors in your kitchen—useful for whacking up bits of parsley for anything from sliced tomatoes to boiled potatoes. Parsley will keep if stored dry in a Mason jar in the refrigerator not too near the freezer. If kept in the hydrator, it always seems to get tangled up like coat hangers in a closet and most of it browns before you can use it. Half an onion, sautéed to translucency in a skillet with a pat of butter, adds greatly to the flavor of this rice. You can also do this with a bell pepper and the children will scarcely notice. Or the weight watchers.

2 cups salted water
1 tablespoon butter or margarine

1 cup rice
1 cup parsley

Combine ingredients and cook 10 minutes at a medium-high boil. Turn off heat and let sit on stove for 30 minutes more.

A salad of grapefruit sections; diced ginger and Bibblettuce—easily grown in Southern gardens in frames—and celery needs no dressing.

POTATO SALAD DELUXE
By George Rector

Potato salad, that worthy running mate of the cold cut and the frank-furter, is very special business requiring forethought and loving care. The term usually means cold sliced potatoes with slabs of raw onion mixed in, the whole mixed with mayonnaise or an old-fashioned boiled dressing. That does all right for a slap-dash dish, but it is to the real thing as a soda cracker is to a hot biscuit. Here is my private method—so far as I know it has never been exhibited before any of the crowned heads of Europe, the few of them that are left, but it should have been. Since I didn't invent it, I can say what I really think of it. I got the idea originally from the technique employed by the best artist in creamed potatoes who ever approached a stove on this side of the Atlantic.

You boil potatoes with their jackets on till tender, then peel them quickly and put them in a bowl. Dive into them with a couple of big forks, stabbing and pulling crosswise until they're all broken up coarse and grainy. Give them our special family French dressing to drink, in proportions of a third of a cup to six medium potatoes and let them marinate—cook's slang for soak. When the French dressing has permeated every atom, throw in a half cup of blanched almonds sliced very thin, a couple of tablespoons of fine chopped onion—a meat grinder does this job without so much eye watering—and another couple of tablespoons of fine-chopped green peppers. Mix it thoroughly and chill it off in the refrigerator. Just before serving, mix in a whole cup of chilled mayonnaise and a tablespoon of fine-chopped parsley, and serve it on lettuce, with paprika sprinkled here and there for garnish. If you like eggs in your salads in general, three or four hard-boiled specimens cut into businesslike chunks introduced along with the onions add both color and flavor. Mutilating your potatoes while they're still hot and "floury" gets rid of that appalling toughness to which the cold boiled potato is generally subject when sliced with a knife. And your cold boiled spuds needn't go to waste because you don't use them in potato salad—cold boiled is the best possible start on hashed brown, and I have yet to meet anybody who looked cross-eyed at hashed brown.

SCALLOPED BARBECUE POTATOES

1½ cups water
½ cup bottled barbecue sauce
1 tablespoon vinegar
1 teaspoon salt
¼ teaspoon pepper

6 medium potatoes (2 pounds),
  peeled and thinly sliced
1 medium onion, thinly sliced
Paprika and chopped parsley

Preheat oven to 350°. In Dutch oven, over medium heat, heat water, barbecue sauce, vinegar, salt and pepper to boiling. Stir in potatoes and onion; simmer 5 minutes, stirring occasionally. Cover and bake 1 hour or until potatoes are tender. Garnish with paprika and chopped parsley. Serve hot or refrigerate several hours to serve cold. Serves 6.
Mrs. John F. Finnegan, *Minneota, Minnesota*

MEAL IN A POTATO

6 large Idaho potatoes
1 cup spinach
¼ cup onion, chopped
½ cup celery, stripped of
  strings and chopped

½ cup carrots, sliced
1 tomato, peeled (no seeds)
1 teaspoon salt
½ cup grated tuna fish
1/3 cup butter or margarine

Wash, dry and grease potatoes. Bake. When done, split lengthwise three-fourths of their length and empty contents into large bowl. Cook spinach, onion, celery, carrots tomato and salt with just enough water to last until tender. Drain, if too much water is left. Add vegetables to tuna fish and margarine and beat on low speed until all is thoroughly mixed. Add half of potatoes which were removed from shells. Refill potato shells and bake 15 minutes in 350° oven. Serve with sour cream and garnish with parsley. Serves 6.
Mary E. Ralph, *Forsyth, Missouri*

VEGETABLE STUFFED POTATOES

3 large baking potatoes
1 (20-ounce) package frozen
  vegetables with cream sauce
2 tablespoons milk

2 tablespoons butter
Salt
Pepper

Scrub potatoes. Place on baking sheet and bake in 400° oven 1 hour or until tender. Meanwhile cook frozen vegetables according to package directions. Halve each potato and scoop out contents. Mash until smooth with 2 tablespoons milk and 2 tablespoons butter. Add seasoning. Next, spoon cooked vegetables into potato shells. Place mashed potatoes on top of vegetables. Return to 400° oven and bake 15 minutes more, or until golden brown. Serves 6.
Mrs. Arthur Baron, *St. Louis, Missouri*

YUMMY YAMMY CRUNCH

2 large cans yams
¼ cup raisins
¼ cup frozen orange juice
   concentrate
1 cup flour

3/4 cup sugar
Dash salt
1½ teaspoons cinnamon
3/4 cup butter
2 cups tiny marshmallows

Place yams and raisins in a buttered 10-by-6-inch baking dish. Pour the orange juice over the yams and raisins. In a medium mixing bowl combine flour, sugar, salt, and cinnamon. Mix well. Cut in the butter until the mixture is coarse. Sprinkle over the yams. Bake at 350° for 30 minutes. Sprinkle with marshmallows. Broil 4 to 5 inches from the broiler until marshmallows are golden brown. Serves 6 to 8.

Joanne Esparcia, *Sacramento, California*

29

HAWAIIAN YAMBROSIA

1 (13¼-ounce) can pineapple
   tidbits
4 slices bacon
1 tablespoon flour
¼ teaspoon salt

¼ teaspoon pepper
1 tablespoon white vinegar
1 (1-pound) can sweet potatoes
1 tablespoon sesame seeds

Drain syrup from pineapple tidbits; measure 3/4 cup (add water if needed). Sauté bacon (which has been cut in small pieces) until crisp. Remove bacon from skillet, leaving 1 tablespoon bacon fat. Stir in flour, salt and pepper. Gradually blend in the reserved pineapple syrup; add vinegar and boil until slightly thick. Slice well-drained sweet potatoes and toss lightly with pineapple tidbits, bacon and sauce. Place in ovenproof serving dish, sprinkle with sesame seeds, and keep warm until serving time. Serves 4 to 6.

Mrs. Clayton Curtis, *Winslow, Indiana*

"For what we are about to receive—with the possible exception of these instant mashed potatoes—we are truly thankful."

MY ITALIAN RICE

Basic Tomato Sauce

3 pounds lean ground beef
   (choice chuck or round)
3 tablespoons bacon fat, oil
   or margarine
3 cups celery, finely cut
3 to 4 large onions, chopped
2 green peppers, chopped
1 (#2½) can tomatoes
1 (#2½) can herb tomatoes
2 small cans tomato with cheese
2 small cans tomato with
   mushrooms
1 large package of dry spaghetti
   sauce mix
½ cup tomato catsup

2 beef bouillon cubes
1 teaspoon Worcestershire sauce
1 teaspoon soy sauce
6 to 8 drops Tabasco sauce
½ package dry onion soup
1½ cups water
½ to 1 cup dry red wine
1/8 teaspoon rosemary
1/8 teaspoon thyme
1 teaspoon oregano
1 teaspoon basil
1 bud of garlic, cut in fourths
1 teaspoon seafood seasoning
½ cup chopped parsley
1 large can mushrooms

3 cups short grain brown rice
   (not instant)
9 cups boiling water
2 teaspoons salt

1 cup mozzarella cheese,
   shredded
1 cup sharp cheddar cheese,
   shredded

Heat Dutch oven over medium burner. Brown beef in bacon fat until light brown and finely chopped. Add celery, onions and peppers. Stir and cook until onions are rather clear. Add remaining sauce ingredients. Cook very slowly at least an hour until all of the fat is floating on top. Fat may be skimmed off. Stir often. Cook rice in boiling water with salt until only partially done. Drain and mix with enough of the sauce so that the mixture is of loose consistency. Mix in mozzarella cheese and cheddar cheese. Pour rice mixture in a 4-quart Dutch oven, sprinkle top generously with Parmesan cheese and bake, covered, in 250° oven for 2 to 3 hours. Rice should be glossy and moist when done, not dry. Tomato sauce may be frozen and used in rice, noodle, lasagne, spaghetti and chili bean recipes. Yield: 4 quarts tomato sauce. Rice serves 10 to 12.

Ruth G. Gleason, *Helena, Montana*

EGGS & CHEESE

Shell Games & Wheys to Your Heart

CHOCOLATE SOUFFLE
By George Bradshaw

Here is the greatest of the dessert soufflés.

In the top of a double boiler melt three tablespoons of butter and mix with three tablespoons of flour. Cook a moment. Then add a cup of milk, stirring constantly until the mixture is rich and creamy.

Add one-half cup of sugar. Stir until dissolved. Add three squares (three ounces) of bitter cooking chocolate, broken into bits. The mixture will appear grainy for a while, but, as you keep stirring, the chocolate will suddenly combine and you will have a smooth, thick, elegant sauce.

Take this off the fire. Add a dash of salt and beat the mixture for a minute. Allow it to cool a bit, then add five beaten egg yolks to it, and beat until smooth.

Beat seven egg whites until stiff. When the chocolate sauce is really cool, take a large spoonful of whites and fold vigorously in the chocolate mixture until it appears slightly foamy. Dribble this sauce over the remaining egg whites, and fold thoroughly and carefully.

Slide all this into a buttered and sugared soufflé dish and place in a 350° oven. At the end of twenty minutes you should have something wonderful. But test it.

Here's a fine, simple sauce to top off the soufflé. Beat a half pint of heavy cream until it's stiff. Allow a half pint of vanilla ice cream to soften—not melt—soften. Then beat these two together. Add a couple of tablespoons of good brandy.

Have yourself a fine dinner with this. Have a roast rolled fillet of beef; have white asparagus; have potatoes Anna. And for a salad, Belgian endive with slices of foie gras *on it and French dressing.*

SWISS MUSHROOM CHEESE PIE
By Clifton Fadiman

For a buffet supper, bake two of these in matching, French, white china baking dishes.

Enough rich pie pastry for 2 crusts in an 8-inch baking dish	4 tablespoons butter
1 pound Swiss cheese, thinly sliced	1 cup thinly sliced mushrooms sautéed in butter
	Light cream

Start oven at hot (425°). Line dish with pastry and chill for ½ hour. Arrange slices of cheese in bottom of lined dish, add dabs of butter and a few mushroom slices. Repeat layers, filling the dish. Cover with pastry and make a decorative crimped edge around the dish. Cut a few gashes in the top layer of pastry. Bake in a hot oven for 20 to 25 minutes; then lower the heat to moderate and bake for 5 or 10 minutes longer, until the pastry is browned. Makes 4 or more servings.

CRAB AND CHEESE SUPREME
By Clifton Fadiman

6 or 8 thin slices bread,
lightly toasted and buttered
2 cups freshly cooked crab meat,
all fibers removed
½ pound Swiss cheese, grated
or cut in thin slivers
3 eggs
1 cup light cream
1 cup milk
Salt, pepper, paprika

Start oven at moderate (325°). Butter an oblong baking-serving dish. Line dish with buttered toast. Cover toast with flaked crab meat. Sprinkle generously with cheese. Beat eggs until light, combine with cream and milk, and pour over contents of dish. Add dash of seasonings. Bake in preheated oven about 50 minutes, or until set. Makes 8 servings.

SWISS AND CAMEMBERT POINTS

4 tablespoons butter
3 ounces ripe Camembert cheese
¼ cup grated Swiss cheese
3 eggs
1 teaspoon salt
Grind of pepper
¼ teaspoon paprika
2 cups all-purpose flour, sifted

Start oven at hot (425°). Grease baking sheet. Cream butter until soft; blend Camembert cheese into butter; add Swiss cheese and beat smooth. Add eggs, one at a time, beating well. Stir salt, pepper and paprika into the flour, sift together, stir into the cheese mixture until soft dough is formed. Pat dough out on a floured board in circle about 10 inches in diameter. Place on prepared baking sheet and cut dough into 16 pie-shaped wedges. Bake for 25 to 30 minutes or until lightly browned. Serve warm or cold with drinks. Makes 16 generous servings.

BAKED CREME LORRAINE

6 slices bacon
1½ cups grated Gruyère cheese
1½ cups grated Parmesan cheese
2 cups heavy cream
2 eggs, well beaten
1 teaspoon salt
½ teaspoon dried basil
Dash pepper and paprika
Toasted French bread

Start oven at moderate (350°). Butter 1½-quart baking dish. Fry bacon until crisp; drain and crumble. Combine bacon, cheese, cream, eggs and seasonings. Pour into baking dish. Place dish in shallow pan of warm water. Bake in preheated moderate oven about 35 minutes or longer, until set. It should be the consistency of thick custard, or slightly firmer. Serve warm, from baking dish, onto toasted French bread. Makes 4 servings.

LASAGNA VERDE

½ cup chopped onion
½ cup chopped celery
½ cup chopped pepper
1 clove garlic, crushed
6 lasagna noodles
1 (12-ounce) package French-cut green beans
1 can cream of mushroom soup

¼ cup chopped parsley
2 teaspoons oregano
1 teaspoon basil
1 egg
1½ cups dry cottage cheese
½ (8-ounce) package mozzarella cheese, cut in 6 slices
1 tablespoon grated Parmesan cheese

34

In large skillet, combine ½ cup water, onion, celery, green pepper and garlic. Cook over medium heat until the vegetables are tender and the water has evaporated (about 10 minutes). Meanwhile cook the noodles and frozen beans as packages direct. Add mushroom soup, beans, parsley, oregano and basil to vegetables. Cook over low heat 5 minutes to blend flavors. Combine egg and cottage cheese in a small bowl, stirring until well blended. Preheat oven to 350°. Place noodles in bottom of 10-by-6-by-2-inch baking dish. Top with one-third of cheese mixture, then one-third of vegetable sauce. Repeat twice. Arrange mozzarella on top; sprinkle with Parmesan cheese. Bake, uncovered, 30 minutes, or until very hot and golden brown. Serves 6.

Betsy P. Dellow, *Winnetka, Illinois*

MADELEINE'S CHEESE SOUFFLE

8 slices white bread
½ pound American cheese
4 eggs
1 cup milk
Salt and pepper

Remove crusts from bread. Place a layer of bread in bottom of buttered round deep casserole. Next, a layer of sliced cheese; a second layer of bread and another layer of cheese. Beat eggs in a bowl and add milk, salt and pepper. Pour egg and milk mixture over bread and cheese in casserole and place in refrigerator at least 3 hours before baking at 350° for 40 minutes.

Mrs. E. L. Lucas, *Washington, D.C.*

MISSION ENCHILADAS

12 flour tortillas
12 slices thin pressed ham
1 pound grated Jack cheese
3 to 4 cans whole green chilis, seeded

White Sauce

½ cup flour
¼ pound soft margarine
1 quart milk
1 pound grated sharp
cheddar cheese
1 teaspoon dry mustard
1 teaspoon salt
¼ teaspoon pepper

To make enchiladas, place one slice of ham on a tortilla. Add some cheese and one chili to the ham and then roll into a tight cone. Melt butter, stir in flour. Add milk and stir until mixture thickens. Add cheese a little at a time until dissolved. Stir slowly. Add mustard, salt and pepper. Pour the sauce over the enchiladas in a buttered 9-by-13-inch baking dish. Bake 45 minutes at 350°. Serves 12.

Pamela Warner, *Mission Viejo, California*

QUICK WELSH RAREBIT

4 ounces cheddar cheese, grated
1 tablespoon catsup
1 teaspoon Worcestershire sauce

Mix above ingredients until well blended. Spread on toasted bread. Melt in oven or broiler. Makes 2 sandwiches.

Mary Grimm, *Baltimore, Maryland*

CAYENNE CHEESE SURPRISES

2 sticks of margarine, softened
2 cups sharp Cheddar Cheese, grated
2 cups flour
2 cups Rice Krispies
2 pinches of salt
2 teaspoons of cayenne

Mix all ingredients together. Form small balls and place on cookie sheet. Flatten and sprinkle lightly with Cayenne. Bake at 375° for 10 to 12 minutes. Watch carefully and cool before removing from the cookie sheet.

Use these appetizers with cocktails or for between meal snacks. They can be made ahead of time and frozen.

Pamela Warner, *Mission Viejo, California*

DUAL-PURPOSE CHEESE RABBIT

1 pound sharp cheese
1 (6-ounce) can tomato paste
1 (10-ounce) can cheddar
  cheese soup
1 teaspoon dry mustard
½ teaspoon Tabasco sauce

½ teaspoon Worcestershire sauce
½ teaspoon salt
½ teaspoon black pepper
½ bottle beer (or 5 ounces
  evaporated milk)

Cut or chop cheese into small thin pieces. Over medium heat, mix beer (or milk), tomato paste, soup, and seasonings until blended. Slowly add pieces of cheese. Continue stirring until all of cheese has been added, and mixture is creamy-thick. Keep warm for serving in a chafing dish, or covered serving dish. Serve over unsalted uneda biscuits, or well-browned toast. [Dual purpose: place leftover rabbit in refrigerator in covered container, to be used as dip for later date, or stuff celery as niblet with hubby's evening meal.] Serves 8.

Mrs. Albert F. Toulotte, *San Francisco, California*

FONDUE DE FROMAGE

2 cups dry white wine
2 garlic cloves, cut up
¾ pound imported, aged Swiss
  cheese, freshly grated (3 cups)
1 tablespoon cornstarch
2 tablespoons butter

2 to 6 tablespoons heavy cream
Salt
Freshly ground black pepper
3 tablespoons kirsch
1 loaf crusty French or Italian
  bread, cut in 1-inch cubes

In 1½-quart saucepan boil the wine and garlic briskly on stove until wine reduces to 1½ cups. Strain through a fine sieve into fondue pot. Discard garlic. Have fondue burner lighted when ready to serve. At stove return wine to a boil. Lower heat and add cheese mixed with cornstarch, stirring constantly. Don't let boil. When cheese is melted and fondue is smooth, stir in butter and 2 tablespoons of the cream. The fondue should be just thick enough to coat a fork heavily. If it seems too thick, add a little more cream, 1 tablespoon at a time. Season with salt and pepper, stir in kirsch and serve at once, at table, accompanied by platter of bread cubes.

Catherine E. Sansone, *Indianapolis Symphony Orchestra, Indianapolis, Indiana*

GRITS AND CHEESE CASSEROLE

4 cups milk
1 cup hominy grits
½ cup butter or margarine
1 roll (6 ounces) garlic cheese

2 eggs, well beaten
½ teaspoon baking powder
¼ teaspoon salt
½ cup grated cheddar cheese

Preheat oven to 375°. Bring 3½ cups milk to boiling point. Gradually stir in grits; cook over medium heat, stirring constantly, until thick—about 10 minutes. Remove from heat. Add butter and garlic cheese; stir until melted. Stir in eggs, baking powder, salt and remaining milk. Pour into 2-quart casserole. Bake, uncovered, 30 minutes, then sprinkle grated cheese over top Bake 15 minutes longer. Makes 6 to 8 servings.

Margaret Hurwitz, *Richmond Heights, Missouri*

BEEF & PORK ENTREES

Meat the Winner

DO AHEAD BEEF STEW
By Mary Alice Sharpe

1 cup hickory smoke
flavored barbecue
sauce
3 pounds beef, cut into
1-inch cubes
1½ cups water
1 teaspoon salt
8 small whole potatoes

8 carrots, cut in
1½-nch pieces
2 celery stalks, cut in
1-inch pieces
1 (16-ounce) jar small
whole onions, drained
1/3 cup cold water
3 tablespoons flour

Pour barbecue sauce over meat. Cover; marinate in refrigerator 3 to 5 hours. Place beef with marinade in Dutch oven; add water and salt. Bring to a boil. Cover; simmer 1 hour. Add vegetables; cover and continue simmering 30 to 45 minutes, or until meat and vegetables are tender. Gradually add flour mixture to hot meat and vegetables, stirring until mixture boils and thickens. Simmer 5 minutes. Makes 8 servings.
NOTE: Stew can be frozen, thawed and heated on an outdoor grill or over a campfire.

HOW TO STY A FRAKE
IN YOUR OUTFIRE DOORPLACE
By Colonel Stoopnagle

Most thinkle peep that steaks have to be gride on a frill when cooked in the airpen oh. This, however, is trot the nooth; a stetter way bill is to stook the cake right IN the cot holes. And here's the days to woo it:

Get a nice, sender turloin. Gub it well with rarrlick. Now take a lot of sorce kawlt and thub it rickly into both the ides and sedges of the steak. Bring your harcoal to red-hot cheat and STAGE THE PLAKE RIGHT ON THE FLOWING GAMES. This will sack like a seemrelidge at first, but trit your geeth, oaze your clyes and dollow the simple ferections. Allow more finnits per three-fourth thinch of ickness per side, and stern the take only once.

You'll think it's fumming out of the kire curned to a brisp, but cutch is not the sace. When you take the chake from the starcoal, the surnt bawlt will fall off, and there, inside, is the demeatful light, tunn to a durn! Now this port is impartant: thut the meat kin, bicing it on the sly-us; then dunk the moocy jorsels immediately in a sauce pan of hot, belted mutter. Rebutt from the moover at once and place on hot, ruttered bowls. Your swests will goon! (Noatitor's Ed: This lessipee is on the revel. I sighed it my-treff!)

GOLDEN BEEF STEW

1½ pounds beef stew meat
¼ cup flour
2 tablespoons shortening
2½ cups hot water
2 tablespoons chopped onion
½ clove garlic
2 teaspoons salt
¼ teaspoon pepper
¼ teaspoon paprika

1/8 teaspoon allspice
1 teaspoon sugar
½ teaspoon lemon juice
½ teaspoon Worcestershire sauce
¼ cup tomato juice
1 cup pearl onions
½ cup carrots, sliced
1 cup potatoes, cubed
½ cup celery, diced

Flour meat and brown in shortening. Add water, chopped onion, garlic, salt, pepper, paprika, allspice, sugar, lemon juice, Worcestershire sauce and tomato juice. Cover and cook over low heat for 2 hours. Add vegetables and cook 15 to 20 minutes longer, or until meat and vegetables are tender. Serves 6.

Mrs. James Volpert, *Peru, Indiana*

HUNGRY FAMILY CASSEROLE

2 (10-ounce) packages frozen
  zucchini or 1 quart fresh
  sliced zucchini
1 pound lean ground beef
1 cup chopped onion
1 clove garlic, crushed
1 teaspoon salt
1 teaspoon basil

½ teaspoon oregano
¼ teaspoon pepper
2 cups cooked rice
1 (8-ounce) can tomato sauce
1 cup small curd cottage cheese
1 egg beaten
1 cup grated cheddar cheese

Cook zucchini in boiling water for 2 to 3 minutes. Drain well. Sauté meat, onion and seasonings until onions are transparent. Stir in rice and tomato sauce. Blend cottage cheese and egg together and add to meat and rice. In buttered 2-quart shallow baking dish arrange half the zucchini slices over bottom of dish. Spoon the meat mixture over half the zucchini. Spread with remaining zucchini. Sprinkle cheddar cheese over all. Bake in 350° oven 20 to 25 minutes until hot and bubbly. Serves 4 to 6.

Mrs. Jean W. Sanderson, *Leawood, Kansas*

CREOLE BEEF

1 tablespoon margarine
1 pound ground beef
1 small onion, chopped
¼ cup chopped green pepper
1 can (#303) whole kernel corn,

drained
1 small can tomato sauce
½ cup grated cheese
¼ teaspoon paprika
Salt and pepper

Brown meat in margarine. Sauté onion and pepper until tender and add to beef. Add remaining ingredients. Stir until cheese melts. Simmer on low heat for 15 minutes. Serves 4.

Mrs. Linda Gray, *Antioch, Tennessee*

BASEBALL DINNER

1½ pounds ground beef
1 small onion, chopped
Salt to taste
Pepper to taste
½ teaspoon chili powder
½ teaspoon celery salt

1 (15-ounce) can Mexican
  chili beans
1 (11½-ounce) can vegetable
  beef soup
1 small can tomato sauce
2 cups cooked egg noodles, drained

In frying pan, brown meat and onion. Add salt, pepper, chili powder and celery salt, mixing well. Drain off excess fat. Add chili beans, vegetable beef soup and tomato sauce. Mix well, let simmer 5 minutes. Fold in egg noodles and heat through. Serves 6.

Mrs. Janice A. Faber, *Boise, Idaho*

BEEF BOURGUIGNON

3 pounds sirloin,
  cut in 2-inch cubes
1½ cups Burgundy wine
2 tablespoons brandy
2 tablespoons salad oil
1 teaspoon salt
½ teaspoon pepper
½ teaspoon thyme
1 bay leaf
6 tablespoons butter

2 cloves of garlic, crushed
2 large onions, chopped
1 carrot, chopped
4 rounded tablespoons flour
1 tablespoon tomato paste
1 cup beef broth
1½ cups tiny white onions
  (1-pound can)
¾ pound mushroom caps

Marinate beef for two hours in wine, brandy, oil, salt, pepper, thyme and bay leaf. Drain, reserving the marinade. Pat meat dry. Brown meat quickly in 2 tablespoons of butter. Remove meat to casserole dish and sauté garlic, onions and carrot until lightly browned in 2 tablespoons butter. Blend in flour and tomato paste. Add marinade and beef broth. Stir until mixture comes to a boil. Pour mixture over meat in casserole. Cover and cook at 350° for 2½ hours. Heat 2 tablespoons butter in skillet. Sauté white onions until golden. Remove. Add mushroom caps and saute for 2 minutes. Place onions and mushrooms on top of casserole and bake 10 minutes more. Serves 6 to 8.

Maureen Nunn, *Palos Verdes Peninsula, California*

MEATBALLS AND CABBAGE

1½ pounds ground chuck
  or hamburger
1 teaspoon salt
¼ teaspoon pepper
½ cup fine cracker crumbs
2 eggs

1 medium head cabbage
1 can tomato soup
1 can water
2 tablespoons sugar
4 thin slices lemon

Combine the hamburger, salt, pepper, cracker crumbs and eggs, and mix
well. Form into 12 balls and set aside. Separate cabbage leaves. Place 1/3 of
leaves loosely in bottom of casserole. Put 6 meatballs on cabbage, then
another layer of leaves, remainder of meatballs, and top with rest of cabbage.
Cover all with tomato soup and water. Sprinkle top with sugar and lemon
slices. Bake at 350° for 1½ hours, adding more water if necessary. Remove
lemon slices before serving. Serves 6.

Mrs. Adolph Silverman, *Dupree, South Dakota*

MEATBALLS RUSSIAN

2 pounds ground beef
2 cups bread crumbs
2 eggs, slightly beaten
½ cup milk
2 tablespoons onion, minced
½ teaspoon garlic powder
1 tablespoon Worcestershire sauce
1 tablespoon grated lemon rind

2 teaspoons salt
White pepper to taste
5 tablespoons butter
2 medium green peppers, chopped
5 tablespoons flour
4 cups canned tomatoes, chopped
2 cups sour cream
Egg noodles

Combine meat, bread crumbs, eggs, milk, onion, garlic powder, Worcestershire sauce, lemon rind, salt and pepper. Shape into balls and brown in 3
tablespoons butter. Place in casserole. Brown green pepper in 2 tablespoons
butter; add flour and cook 1 minute. Add canned tomatoes, and sour cream,
stirring until thick and smooth. Pour creamed mixture over meatballs. Bake
at 300° for 45 to 60 minutes. Serve with buttered egg noodles. Serves 8.

M. L. Savidge, *Fair Oaks, California*

GRAND HAM SLAM CASSEROLE

2½ cups cooked ham, diced
1 (10½-ounce) can cream of
  asparagus soup
1 cup broccoli tips, snipped
  from stalks
1 medium-size onion, diced fine
1 egg, whipped to a froth

1 cup creamed cottage cheese,
  whipped
¼ teaspoon black pepper
2 teaspoons garlic juice
3 teaspoons cider vinegar
1 teaspoon prepared mustard

Blend all ingredients in 1½-quart casserole. Bake at 350° for 45 minutes.
Garnish with fresh orange slices or winter pears. Serve over bed of bulgur
wheat or rice pilaf. Serves 6.

Kathy Sparks, *Menlo Park, California*

HAM AND NOODLE CASSEROLE

4 ounces medium noodles
1 can condensed cream of
  celery soup
½ cup milk
½ teaspoon prepared mustard

¼ teaspoon salt
1½ cups mixed cooked vegetables
1 cup cubed cooked ham
2 hard-cooked eggs, quartered
Buttered bread crumbs

Cook noodles. Combine the soup, milk, mustard and salt. Mix well. Fold in
the noodles, vegetables and ham. Put in casserole; place eggs on top. Sprinkle
with bread crumbs. Cook 30 minutes at 350°. Serves 4.

Mrs. H. Rauscher, *South Farmingdale, New York*

"Having hash again, eh?"

HAM PINWHEEL CASSEROLE

Dough:

1½ cups prepared biscuit mix
½ cup yellow cornmeal
1¼ ounces taco seasoning sauce

½ cup grated cheddar cheese
½ cup milk

Filling:

2½ cups thinly sliced ready-cooked
  ham, shredded

2 tablespoons chopped pimiento
2 tablespoons chopped black olives

Spicy Pineapple Sauce:

1 cup condensed cheddar cheese
  soup undiluted
1 cup pineapple juice

1/8 teaspoon paprika
½ teaspoon dry mustard
½ cup commercial sour cream

Mix the biscuit mix, cornmeal and taco seasoning sauce. Toss in the grated
cheese with a fork. Add milk and mix to a dough consistency. Roll on lightly
floured board to 10- by 14-inch rectangle. Mix shredded ham with pimiento
and olives and scatter evenly over the dough. Roll up jelly-roll style from the
long side. Seal the edges and ends. Cut into 8 slices and place slices cut side
down in a greased 10½-by-6½-inch baking dish. Bake at 450° until browned
and dough is cooked—about 25 minutes. In a saucepan mix the cheese soup
with the pineapple juice, paprika and dry mustard. Cook until hot, stirring
constantly. Gently stir in the sour cream. Serve the rolls individually and
pass the hot pineapple sauce around separately to be used by diners as they
desire. Serves 4.

Mrs. Morris Grout, *Marysville, Washington*

HAM ROLL WITH YAMMY FILLING

3 cups mashed sweet potatoes
  (or yams)
Salt, pepper, and dash of nutmeg
2 tablespoons butter
½ pound ground ham
¼ pound ground beef

½ pound pork sausage
2 tablespoons milk
2 eggs
½ cup bread crumbs
2 strips bacon, cut in half

Season mashed yams with salt, pepper, nutmeg and butter. Form a roll about
8 inches long and wrap in wax paper. Chill thoroughly. Combine the meats
with milk, beaten eggs, and bread crumbs; mix well and turn onto wax
paper. Pat meat into a rectangle 8 inches wide. Place yam mixture in center
and wrap meat around it, pressing edges firmly together. Place in baking pan,
strip with bacon, and bake at 350° for 1 hour. Serves 8.

Mrs. Mary A. Finnegan, *Minneota, Minnesota*

PLUM-PLEASING PORK ROAST

1 (5- to 6-pound) pork roast,
  well trimmed
1 bottle Italian salad dressing
2 (#2½) cans purple plums
1 (6-ounce) can frozen lemonade

concentrate
1 teaspoon soy sauce
1 teaspoon ground ginger
1 (6-ounce) package slivered
  almonds

Marinate pork roast in Italian dressing for 3 hours. Drain plums, reserving 1 cup syrup. Seed plums. Puree in a blender or through a sieve. Add reserved plum syrup, lemonade, soy sauce and ginger. Mix well. Remove roast from marinade and place in 350° oven for 1½ hours. Spoon 3 or 4 tablespoons of plum mixture over roast every 15 minutes for the next hour. Just before removing from the oven, add remaining plums and broil for a minute. Slice pork in thin slices, spoon small amount of sauce on each slice, and top with slivered almonds. Serves 10.

Caryol Coryell, *Boise, Idaho*

ROBIN HOOD PORK CASSEROLE

6 large, thick pork chops
1 cup applesauce
2 tablespoons onion soup mix

1 cup cranberries or 1 (16-ounce)
  can whole-berry cranberry sauce
  (not the jellied)

Brown chops in frying pan. Put applesauce and onion soup mix in 2-quart casserole. Add chops and cranberries to casserole. Cover and bake in 325° for 1½ hours. Serves 6.

Mrs. Elizabeth B. Fitzgerald, *Springfield, Massachusetts*

SMOKED PORK CASSEROLE

1 cup rice
1 cup beef broth
1 cup water
1 medium onion, chopped
2 tablespoons butter
1 (10-ounce) package frozen
  lima beans
2 cups cooked, smoked pork,
  cut into bite-size pieces
4 small or 3 large tomatoes,

peeled, seeded and chopped
(or 1½ pounds canned tomatoes,
peeled, drained and chopped)
1 (8-ounce) can tomato sauce
1 teaspoon Worcestershire sauce
1/3 cup sherry
1 tablespoon shredded basil
  (or 1 teaspoon dried basil)
Salt and pepper to taste

Cook rice in beef broth and water, according to package directions. Sauté the chopped onion in butter until yellow. Cook lima beans according to package directions. Combine the cooked pork, rice, lima beans, chopped tomatoes and sautéed onion in layers in a casserole dish. Mix together the tomato sauce, Worcestershire sauce, sherry, basil, salt and pepper and pour over the layered ingredients. Bake in 350° oven for 30 minutes. Serves 4.

Mrs. Martha Swanson, *Killingworth, Connecticut*

SULLY'S BARBECUED PORK RIBS

2 to 3 racks pork ribs
Salt
Coarse ground black pepper
1 cup red wine vinegar
3 medium onions, minced
1 clove mashed garlic

3 tablespoons dry mustard
6 tablespoons brown sugar
½ teaspoon Tabasco
2 cups catsup
2 lemons (good quality rind),
   thinly sliced

Choose lean, meaty ribs, preferably with the backbone portion still attached. Cut racks into pieces: 3 to 4 ribs per portion. Salt and pepper ribs on both sides. Combine in a blender remaining ingredients, except catsup and lemons and blend. Pour into saucepan. Add catsup mixture and simmer for 15 to 20 minutes after first bubbles appear. When bubbling commences, add thinly sliced lemons. Stir occasionally to prevent sticking.

Using a barbecue grill with a low but evenly distributed bed of coals, brown ribs on one side, then turn and baste liberally with a brush, including section edges. Continue to turn and baste frequently for about 90 minutes.

Remove ribs from the grill when most of the fat has disappeared. Separate sections into individual ribs. Place them edge up in roaster and paint each layer with remaining sauce and lemon slices. Put covered roaster in a 250° oven for 45 minutes.

Captain R. S. Sullivan, SC, USN(RET), *Miami, Missouri*

45

"He wants that hamburger edible, whatever that means."

HARVEST-TIME CASSEROLE

1 head cabbage, shredded (6 cups)
1 teaspoon salt
12 soda crackers
1 cup milk
½ pound bacon, fried or broiled
   until crisp
2 cups barbecue-flavored potato
   chips, crushed
1 tablespoon butter
½ cup brown sugar
1 tablespoon flour
2 medium McIntosh apples
1 package smoked sausages

Cook shredded cabbage in small amount of boiling water 5 to 10 minutes, until cabbage is limp but not completely cooked. Stir occasionally to assure even cooking. Add salt. Place half of cabbage in bottom of 2-quart casserole. Sprinkle crushed crackers over top of cabbage. Pour on ½ cup milk. Add layer of crushed bacon. Place remainder of salted cabbage in the casserole. Add remaining ½ cup milk. Sprinkle crushed potato chips over the top. Cream butter, brown sugar and flour; mix with cored and diced apple. Distribute on top of cabbage. Arrange smoked sausages on top of casserole and bake, covered, in 375° oven for 45 minutes. Remove cover for an additional 15 minutes. Serves 4.

Mary E. Scott, *Central Lake, Michigan*

SWEDISH MEATBALL STEW

1 pound ground pork (not pork
   sausage)
2 slices bread, crumbled
1 egg
1 package onion soup mix
Scant ¼ teaspoon allspice
¼ to ½ cup milk
1 can chicken broth
   plus ½ can water
3 large carrots
2 medium potatoes
1 medium head cabbage

Mix first 5 ingredients together, adding milk slowly until soft but not sloppy. Roll into small balls and brown gently in a 5-quart Dutch oven or large pan. Pour can of chicken broth over meatballs. Scrub carrots and cut diagonally into chunks. Peel and cut 2 potatoes into chunks. Add vegetables to meatballs and simmer gently for ½ hour. Chop cabbage into large chunks and add. Simmer together until cabbage is just barely fork tender. If desired, broth may be thickened slightly by mixing 1 tablespoon flour in ¼ cup water. Shake in plastic shaker and add to mixture, stirring for at least 5 minutes. Serves 4.

Mrs. Helen Woods, *Santa Monica, California*

POULTRY

For the Birdwatchers

CHICKEN CASSEROLE

2 cans chicken noodle soup
1 can mushroom soup
2 eggs
1 package of Stove Top stuffing
(prepared according to package
directions)

2 cooked chicken breasts, cubed
¾ stick margarine, melted
½ cup of crushed cornflakes mixed
with the remaining ¼ stick of
margarine

Mix the first 6 ingredients and place in a buttered casserole. Top with the cornflake mixture and bake in a 350° oven for 1 hour. Serves 4.

Mrs. A.R. Schultz, *Redlands, California*

CHICKEN EL CAPITAN

1 (4- to 5-pound) stewing hen,
cut up
1 can condensed cream of chicken
soup
2 teaspoons salt
½ teaspoon pepper
1 tablespoon lemon juice

2 tablespoons minced onion
½ cup chopped asparagus
6 pitted ripe olives, chopped
½ cup chopped celery
2 tablespoons flour
2 cups milk

Wash and prepare chicken pieces. Cover with cold water and cook on top of stove about 30 to 45 minutes. When tender enough, remove chicken meat from bones, place chicken meat in 2-quart casserole and add soup, salt and pepper. Stir until smooth. Add lemon juice, onion, asparagus, olives and celery. Cook until vegetables are tender, about 30 minutes. Add flour and milk, stirring until smooth and desired thickness for sauce. Heat until bubbly. Serves 6.

Mary Garner, *St. Petersburg, Florida*

CREOLE COUNTRY BAKE

2 pounds chicken breasts
1/3 cup flour
1/3 cup butter or margarine
2 pounds cleaned shrimp

(thaw if frozen)
1 (20-ounce) package frozen mixed
vegetables, thawed

Sauce Ingredients:

½ cup dry white wine—Sauterne
2 cups canned tomatoes
¼ teaspoon celery seed
¼ teaspoon hot sauce

2 teaspoons salt
½ teaspoon oregano
1 clove garlic, chopped fine

Skin chicken breasts and remove meat from bones; cut into 1½-inch cubes. Dredge meat chunks with flour. Heat butter or margarine in heavy skillet; brown chicken cubes until golden. Place meat in a 4-quart casserole; add shrimp and mixed vegetables, tossing lightly to mix. Add all sauce ingredients to drippings in skillet. Heat, scraping up browned bits from bottom of the pan. When mixture begins to bubble around the edges, pour sauce over ingredients in casserole. Cover casserole tightly and bake in preheated 350° oven for 45 to 50 minutes or until shrimp and chicken are tender. Serve with hot steamed rice. Serves 6 to 8.

Mrs. Selma Albrecht, *Minneapolis, Minnesota*

FARE GAME IN CABBAGE ROLL

4 Cornish game hens
  (or quail, partridge or squab)
4 cups shredded cabbage
4 small carrots, thinly sliced
4 slices bacon, cut in 1-inch pieces,
  crisply fried and drained
2 tablespoons butter or margarine,

melted
¼ teaspoon caraway seed
16 cabbage leaves
1 cup chicken broth
½ teaspoon crushed tarragon leaves
¼ teaspoon thyme

Preheat oven to 350°. Sprinkle birds inside and out with salt and pepper to suit taste. Combine next 5 ingredients; spoon a fourth into each cavity of birds. Wrap each bird in 4 cabbage leaves; secure with string. Place birds in deep casserole; add remaining ingredients and cover. Bake 45 to 60 minutes or until tender. Remove string and cabbage leaves. Serve with pan juices. Makes 4 servings.

Mrs. Lucille Bredy, *Homedale, Idaho*

MOZZARELLA CHICKEN AND LINGUINE CASSEROLE

3 gloves crushed garlic
1 tablespoon salad oil
1 to 2 pounds boneless chicken
1 pound linguine
16 ounces tomato sauce

¼ cup hot water
4 ounces sliced, drained
  mushrooms
Salt and pepper
4 ounces mozzarella cheese

Brown garlic in hot oil. Cook chicken 3 minutes on each side in oil. Cook linguine. Wash and drain it. Mix tomato sauce, hot water and mushrooms in a bowl. Salt and pepper to taste. Add the following to casserole dish: 1/3 sauce mixture, drained linguine, 1/3 sauce mixture, chicken, sauce mixture, mozzarella cheese. Bake in oven 20 to 25 minutes at 325°. Serves 6.

Rosalyn Segal, *Cambridge, Massachusetts*

THOROUGHLY MODERN CHICKEN LIVERS

2 pounds chicken livers
2 cups mushroom caps (large)
1 pineapple, peeled, cored,
  cut in half, each half to be cut
  in 16 wedges
1 cup chicken bouillon

2 tablespoons soy sauce
2 tablespoons salad oil
2 tablespoons lemon juice
½ teaspoon garlic powder
1 tablespoon sugar

Slice mushroom caps and chicken livers in half. Alternately lay chicken livers, mushroom caps and pineapple wedges on bottom of 2-quart oven-proof casserole dish. Combine chicken bouillon, soy sauce, salad oil, lemon juice, garlic powder and sugar. Pour over each layer of chicken, mushrooms and pineapple. Bake at 350° for 10 to 12 minutes. Serves 4.

Ensign Richard O'Brien, *Detroit, Michigan*

TIJUANA POLENTA

1 cup yellow cornmeal
1 cup cold water
4 chicken bouillon cubes
3 cups hot water
Butter or margarine to grease
  casserole

2 cups cold cooked chicken, cubed
1 (6-ounce) bottle hot taco sauce
3 cups hot half-and-half
½ pound Monterey Jack cheese,
  shredded

Stir the cornmeal into the cold water. Dissolve the bouillon cubes in the hot water and add the wet cornmeal. Cook, stirring constantly, until it draws away from the side of the pan. Butter a deep casserole or baking pan. Spread the polenta (cooked cornmeal) in the casserole. Sprinkle in the cold chicken cubes; pour on the sauce, then the cream. Lastly, sprinkle the cheese over all. Bake at 350° about 45 minutes, or until the cheese is melted and slightly brown. Use as a main dish. Serves 6.

Avis M. Alishouse, *Akron, Colorado*

"How did you enjoy your dinner, sir?"

50

CHICK-'N-CHILADAS

1 clove garlic, minced
2 tablespoons salad oil
1 (12-ounce) can tomatoes
(1½ cups)
2 cups chopped onion
2 (4-ounce) cans mild green chilis,
seeded and chopped
1 teaspoon garlic salt

½ teaspoon oregano
½ cup water
3 cups bite-size cooked chicken
2 cups grated Monterey Jack cheese
2 cups sour cream
1/3 cup shortening
1 package corn tortillas (15)

51

Cook garlic in salad oil until tender. Add tomatoes, onion, green chilis, garlic salt, oregano and ½ cup water. Cook over low heat until thickened. Combine chicken, cheese and sour cream; mix. Heat shortening. Dip tortillas just enough to make limp; drain. Fill tortillas with chicken mixture; roll up. Place open side down in baking dish. Spoon tomato mixture over top. Bake at 325° for 15 minutes or until hot through. Makes 15.

Joel Allard, *San Antonio, Texas*

CORNISH CASSEROLE

4 Cornish hens
2 cups bread crumbs
4 teaspoons dried salad herbs
½ teaspoon salt
¼ teaspoon pepper
1½ cups Sauterne wine

½ pint sour cream
1 (4-ounce) can mushroom bits
and pieces, drained
1 (16-ounce) can boiled onions,
drained
½ cup melted butter

Cut each hen in half and wipe dry. Combine bread crumbs, herbs, salt and pepper. Dip hens into wine and then coat with bread crumb mix. Place on wax paper. Combine wine, sour cream and remaining crumb mixture. Grease a 2- to 3-quart baking dish. Spoon crumb mixture into dish and spread around. Cover with mushrooms and onions. Place hens on top of ingredients and pour melted butter over all. Bake at 350° for 60 to 70 minutes or until hens are tender. Serves 4.

Mrs. Marilyn Uhl, *Clyde, Ohio*

BREASTS OF CHICKEN VICHYSSOISE

3 whole broiler-fryer
chicken breasts, halved
½ teaspoon salt
½ cup pancake mix
½ teaspoon garlic salt

¼ cup margarine, melted
1 (13-ounce) can vichyssoise soup
1 tablespoon freeze-dried chives
¼ cup Sauterne wine

Sprinkle chicken breasts with salt. Put pancake mix and garlic salt into a small plastic bag and shake chicken pieces in it to coat. Melt the margarine in a casserole or baking dish large enough to hold chicken in a single layer, and roll the skin side of the chicken in it to coat; then turn pieces skin side up. Bake at 425° until chicken is lightly browned. Mix together soup, chives and wine and pour over chicken. Cover and bake at 350° for about 35 minutes, or until chicken is fork tender. Serves 3 to 6.

Georgia Dotson, *Washington, D.C.*

CHICKEN PETIT

1 large onion
1 clove garlic
3 tablespoons cooking oil
4 cooked chicken breasts,
  each in quarters
1 cup white rice

1 cup water
1 (15-ounce) can dark red kidney
  beans
½ packet of taco seasoning
2 ounces cream of coconut

Sauté onion and 1 sliced garlic clove in cooking oil. Quickly stir-fry chicken in 12-inch skillet; brown lightly. Remove chicken to platter. Add to remaining onion and garlic in skillet 1 cup rice, 1 cup water and can of kidney beans plus taco seasoning. Cover tightly and cook over low heat for approximately 20 minutes. After 10 minutes you may need additional small amount of water (or white wine). When rice is almost ready, add diced chicken and coconut cream to skillet. Cover and cook additional 10 minutes. Serve piping hot with green salad and corn bread. Serves 6.
Mrs. Marianne J. Whitney, *New City, New York*

CHICKEN SUPERB

1 plump fryer, cut into pieces,
  or 5 plump chicken breasts
1 teaspoon salt
4 tablespoons butter
1½ cups seasoned poultry stuffing
1 (10-ounce) can condensed
  cream of mushroom soup

½ cup sliced mushrooms
½ cup sliced, pitted black olives
1 small jar sliced pimientos
½ cup chicken broth
1 (16-ounce) can French-style
  green beans

Place chicken pieces in small saucepan. Cover with water; add salt and 2 tablespoons butter. Simmer until meat is tender. Remove from heat; cut from bones and chop into large cubes. Place in 1½-quart casserole. Add 2/3 cup of stuffing, mushroom soup, mushrooms, olives, and pimientos. Pour chicken broth over mixture and toss lightly. Add beans and toss again, mixing ingredients well. Sprinkle remaining stuffing over top. Place thin pats of remaining butter over top of stuffing. Sprinkle liberally with water. Bake in 350° oven for 30 minutes, or until casserole begins to bubble. Garnish with parsley. Serves 6 to 8.
Susan Gibson Rainey, *Weldon, North Carolina*

NANA'S CHICKEN

1 (2¼- to 3¼-pound)
  quartered chicken
¼ cup flour
½ teaspoon salt
¼ teaspoon pepper
1 teaspoon paprika

¼ cup butter
1 cup cream of
  chicken soup
1 (3- or 4-ounce) can sliced,
  undrained mushrooms
1 tablespoon sherry

Combine flour, salt, pepper and paprika. Place in bag with chicken and shake to coat. Melt butter in shallow casserole. Add chicken (skin-side down). Bake in 400° oven for 30 minutes. Turn chicken. Combine and heat chicken soup, mushrooms and sherry. Pour over chicken and bake 15 to 30 minutes longer, or until tender. Yield: 4 servings.
Mrs. June Eberbach, *Indianapolis, Indiana*

FISH
The Ones That Didn't Get Away

SEAFOOD WITH A SOUTHERN ACCENT
By George Rector

Southern seafood traditions will bear a good deal of investigating all right. New England and Louisiana have had plenty of play from itinerant epicures, but there is a long stretch of seashore and imaginative cookery in between. Maryland terrapin, for instance, is adequately famous, but few outsiders have ever experienced what a Carolina cook can do with a "slider"—the local name for ordinary turtle—and I never yet met anybody who had ever heard of, let alone experimented with, the Florida cracker's habit of eating the weird animals which inhabit conch shells. We don't even have to move outside Charleston to find another rib-sticking version of an easily available shellfish. Did you ever have a Carolina shrimp pie?

It isn't a pie at all, being totally innocent of crust, but there's never any point in being pedantic. Fresh shrimp, boiled and shucked, is the best possible beginning, but good canned shrimp will do all right. Two pounds will work out to feed four people to the danger point. If the shrimps are big, cut them in two. Then chop up a small onion and fry it light brown in two tablespoons of butter in a frying pan along with a chopped-up green pepper. Crumble three slices of stale white bread into an ordinary-sized can of tomatoes, mix in the shrimps, all pink and innocent, season them discreetly with pepper and salt and two tablespoons of chili sauce, and then introduce the whole into the frying pan, to be cooked slowly along with the onion for twenty minutes. Three hard-cooked eggs pretty well chopped up join the party at this point, and then everything is poured into a greased baking dish, covered with fine dry bread crumbs, dotted with butter for a richener and softener. Fifteen minutes in a moderate oven will brown the crumbs and produce a magnificent swamp of mingled this and that underneath. It's as rich as the mud in a Sea Island rice plantation, and illustrates the why of the local proverb that Charleston lives on tourists in the winter and shrimps in the summer. With minor variations for stepping the liquid content either up or down, the same layout will do equally well for oysters, crab meat, lobster meat, scallops, and so forth.

HOW TO MAKE A DOWN-EAST LOBSTER STEW
By Samuel T. Williamson

Boil two one-pound lobsters, preferably female, for fifteen minutes. Slit the lobsters open on a flat pan so as to save the juice. Remove tomalley, any coral roe and all meat, including that from the big claws. Squeeze juice from each small claw. Put meat, juice, tomalley and roe in a pan with one-third cup of melted butter. Stir so that each piece is buttered, cover and let stand for about four hours. Heat a quart and a half of light cream in a double boiler to just below the scalding point, then add buttered lobster meat and juice, a quarter teaspoon of sodium glutamate, one teaspoon Maggi liquid flavoring, and, if extra coloring is wanted, a quarter teaspoon of paprika. If necessary, salt to taste, although in most cases the butter and salty juice should be sufficient. When the mixture is cool, put in refrigerator for at least twenty-four hours. Reheat before serving, adding a couple of tablespoons of sherry if desired. Serves six.

OUTDOOR OYSTER ROAST
By Roy Andries de Groot

This requires a large, flat, open, iron pan, balanced over the fire. (I use a Spanish paella, 18 inches across.) Since "roasting" is very quick, first prepare all ingredients. Scrub and wash 3 dozen oysters, or more. Melt, in smallish iron pan, ½ pound butter and keep lukewarm. Coarsely grate ½ cup shelled pecans. Get large open pan spitting hot. Quickly lay on oysters, hollow shell downward. Cover at once with soaking wet burlap sacking. This involves much hissing and steam. Heat butter until it starts sizzling, add grated pecans and stir until darkish brown, being careful not to let them burn. Then add, in one measure, 2 teaspoons tarragon wine vinegar. Sauce will froth violently. Stir once and remove from fire. After about 4 or 5 minutes, lift edge of burlap covering and, with tongs, remove each oyster that has opened sufficiently for a knife to be inserted. Discard flat top shell and serve oysters, with pecan sauce spooned over each.

CLAMBAKE

Buy sweet and white baking potatoes, a few pounds of yellow onions, 2 or 3 ears of corn and 1 small lobster per person. At the beach, immediately organize hunting forces for razor and surf clams, cherrystones, mussels, bay scallops and crabs. Start surf casting for fish. Above the high-water mark dig a trench 2 feet deep, 3 feet wide and 6 feet long. Line the trench with smooth rocks, fill with dry wood and start the fire about 3½ hours before you wish to eat. To clean clams and mussels, scrub and soak in a bucket of sea water to which have been added several handfuls of flour. Wash potatoes, husk corn and wrap each in foil. Clean lobsters and crabs. Cut cleaned fish into chunks, sandwich between onion slices and foil-wrap. After about 2½ hours when the fire dies down to a white-hot and smokeless bed, cover it with a 6-inch blanket of wet rockweed covered with sackcloth soaked in sea water. Vary and spread assorted food interspersed with onions on the cloth in an even layer. Cover with more wet sackcloth, another 6-inch blanket of wet rockweed and over all place a heavy canvas tarpaulin weighted with stones to seal in the steam. Allow about 1 hour for the cooking. Then unroll the tarpaulin from one end and take out only enough food for the first serving. Serve with melted butter in dipping bowls.

PAN-FRIED TROUT WITH EGGS

Allow ¾ pound trout per serving. Clean (leaving on heads and tails), wash, dry, and lightly coat with cornmeal. Break 8 eggs into bowl, add 1 table-spoon finely cut chives and beat lightly. Melt 5 ounces butter in frying pan and put in trout. Brown on both sides for about 10 minutes, then add salt and pepper. Remove fish to a warm dish. Melt another 5 ounces butter and gently stir in ¾ pint heavy cream. Stir continually until sauce has boiled down to the consistency of light cream. Pour half over fish. Give eggs a final beat, then slosh into pan and scramble over gentle heat. Spoon eggs alongside fish and serve garnished with watercress.

OYSTERS LONGCHAMPS
AND OYSTER STEW
By George Rector

It was probably my pride in handling oysters with loving care that helped reconcile me to our fancy oyster dishes at the old place—oysters Longchamps, for instance. It's a fine thing to do with bulk oysters in the home. That remark back there about oysters out of a paper bucket was not intended as a slur on anything or anybody but the soulless restaurateur who tries to fake half-shell service, you understand.

A big frying pan is the first field of action for oysters Longchamps. Melt a couple of tablespoons of butter in it and cook in the butter for a few minutes a couple of small white onions minced fine and a half cup of chopped mushrooms. Then thicken that with a couple of tablespoonfuls of flour by patient degrees to avoid lumps. When the mixture reaches a boil, toss in two tablespoons of sherry, a half teaspoon of salt and a few grains of cayenne—all of which makes a very pretty background for an oyster's rich subtleties. Enter the oysters, a full pint of them, plus a tablespoon of chopped parsley—step down the heat before the oysters are put in. They cook in the mixture for just one minute and then the whole business is poured into a shallow casserole, covered with buttered bread crumbs and baked brown in a moderate oven. In the face of that bland creamy deliciousness, it's hard to maintain that oysters should never be cooked. The same holds good for old-fashioned oyster dressing for roast chicken and roast turkey.

If we must cook oysters, however, I can be blinded and backed into an oyster stew without much trouble. The proper way of making an oyster stew is a sort of elementary education in the cooking of oysters in general.

Don't let an unworthy hankering after richness at all costs trick you into making one of those all-cream stews—hot cream is a fine thing for coffee, as they serve it in Vienna, but for any other purpose, it's always sickly rich. The prescription here is two parts of milk to one of cream—not even half and half. Eight oysters to a portion is adequately generous, to be planted in a saucepan with a quarter cup of the oyster liquor, a dash of cayenne, a pinch of salt and, if you fancy the effect, a generous pinch of celery salt. Bring that to a quick boil and give it just a minute of boiling. Then skim the top and put in the milk-and-cream mixture, which should be hot, but not have been allowed to boil. Turn up the fire and stir a little and, just as it reaches a boil again, throw in a tablespoon of butter. Paprika sprinkles prettily over the top, and the oyster crackers, which should of course be served with the stew, are to be floated and pursued by the spoon, no matter what the book of etiquette says.

SCRAMBLED CLAMS AND EGGPLANT EN CASSEROLE

1 eggplant (about 6 inches long)
½ teaspoon salt
1 (6-ounce) can minced clams
1 cup milk
2 tablespoons minced onion
2 tablespoons butter or margarine
1½ tablespoons flour
2 tablespoons chopped parsley
½ cup boiled mushrooms
1/8 teaspoon garlic powder
1 tablespoon Worcestershire sauce
½ cup soft bread crumbs

Cut peeled eggplant into cubes and boil in small amount of salted water. Drain clams, and add to eggplant. Combine milk and clam liquid. Sauté minced onion in 1 tablespoon butter. Add flour, milk, and clam liquid to saucepan and when sauce boils, add parsley, mushrooms, garlic powder, Worcestershire sauce, clams and eggplant. Bake in greased 1½-quart casserole at 325° for 35 minutes. Sprinkle top with bread crumbs and remaining butter. Serves 4.

Jean S. Bailey, *Saratoga, California*

SHORE AND COUNTRY CLAM PIE

4 (6½-ounce) cans minced sea clams
1 pound fresh mushrooms
3 tablespoons margarine or butter
4 or 5 dashes of pepper
1 teaspoon Worcestershire sauce
1 cup clam liquid
1 cup sour cream
2 tablespoons flour
Pastry for 2-crust 9-inch pie
3 tablespoons clam liquid for pie top

Drain clams, SAVE all liquid. Clean and coarse-chop mushrooms to same size as clam pieces. In 10- or 12-inch covered frying pan, cook chopped mushrooms in margarine. Add pepper and Worcestershire sauce. Remove cover, and cook away most of juice. Reduce heat. In separate pan, boil 1 cup clam liquid down to ½ cup. Add concentrated clam liquid to mushrooms. (Total liquid should appear to be a generous ½ cup when pan is tipped away from mushrooms.) Add sour cream to mushrooms. Add flour to clams and mix. Add floured clams to mushrooms. Stir until thickened and remove from heat. Spoon clam-mushroom filling into pie shell. Cover with well-slashed top crust. Sprinkle the 3 tablespoons clam juice over top crust of unbaked pie. Bake in preheated 450° oven for 10 to 15 minutes. Reduce heat to 400° and bake 30 minutes longer or until pie is golden brown and bubbly. Serves 6.

Mrs. William H. Walsh, *Bay Village, Ohio*

CHANNEL CAT, "SHOW-ME" STYLE

2 channel catfish (1 to 2
   pounds each)
Salt
Pepper
Garlic powder
2 lemons (1 for each fish)
Oregano
Paprika
1 tablespoon butter (per fish)

Place fish on aluminum foil. Sprinkle generously with salt, pepper and garlic powder on each side. Grate the rind of one lemon on each fish. Then squeeze the juice of one lemon on each fish. Add a pinch of oregano and dust on both sides with paprika. Dot with butter. Seal aluminum foil with a drugstore wrap so juices do not leak out. Bake in a 350° oven for 45 minutes to one hour, depending on the size of the fish. Serves 4.

Mrs. Gay Schroer, *St. Peters, Missouri*

COD FISH CASSEROLE

1 package frozen codfish
1 teaspoon seasoned salt
6 servings instant mashed potatoes
½ pound salt pork, diced
1 tablespoon butter
1 medium green pepper, sliced
1 small onion, diced

½ cup celery, sliced
1 can cream of celery soup
 (undiluted)
8 ounces fresh mushrooms, sliced
1 package (8-ounce) cooked
 salad shrimp

Season codfish with salt. Wrap in foil and bake 30 minutes at 350°. Drain excess juice and flake. Set aside. Prepare instant mashed potatoes, making them stiff. Set aside. Fry salt pork which has been diced, until crisp. Drain off grease. Add butter, green papper, onion and celery and cook until onion is clear using medium to low heat. Add celery soup, mushrooms and shrimp. Line 12-inch oval casserole with mashed potatoes. Place fish and shrimp mixture in center. Bake in 400° oven for 15 to 20 minutes (until piping hot). Serve garnished with alternate slices of fresh tomatoes and green peppers. Serves 4 to 6.

Mrs. Cletus A. Bille, *Huron, Ohio*

FISH "BATES" CASSEROLE

2 stalks celery
1 to 2 medium onions
2 pounds fresh or frozen fish fillets
 (cod, flounder, or fillets of your
 choice)
Basic recipe for white sauce (butter,
 flour, milk and seasonings)
½ cup dry white sherry wine

 (optional)
Juice of ½ lemon
Paprika
2 to 3 tablespoons Parmesan cheese
Salt and pepper
½ cup prepared bread stuffing mix
3 tablespoons slivered almonds

Line greased oblong shallow baking dish with diced celery and onions. Use enough to cover bottom of baking dish. Place fillets on top of celery and onions. Spoon white sauce mixture over fillets. If wine is used, add to white sauce. Sprinkle with lemon juice, paprika and Parmesan cheese. Season with salt and pepper. Sprinkle with bread stuffing and almonds. Bake at 350° for 30 to 35 minutes or until fish flakes easily. Serves 6.

Mrs. James C. Bates, *Chamblee, Georgia*

THREE-MINUTE TUNA-SPINACH CASSEROLE

1 (7-ounce) can tuna
1 (10-ounce) package frozen
 chopped spinach, thawed
1/3 cup fine dry bread crumbs
3 tablespoons herb seasoned
 stuffing

1 tablespoon lemon juice
¼ teaspoon salt
½ cup mayonnaise
3 tablespoons Parmesan
 cheese, grated

Combine all ingredients in casserole. Sprinkle with additional cheese. Bake at 350° in preheated oven for 20 to 25 minutes. Serve plain or over cooked rice. Serves 4 to 6.

Mrs. Michael Gutshall, *Totowa, New Jersey*

DOWN EAST FISH CHOWDER

¼ pound salt pork, diced
2 medium onions, sliced or diced
1 small whole onion
4 cups raw potatoes, cut in small
   pieces
1 cup or more of water
2 to 3 pounds haddock fillets

1 teaspoon salt
¼ teaspoon black pepper
Pinch of thyme
1 quart of whole milk
1 small can evaporated milk
1 to 3 tablespoons butter

Fry diced salt pork slowly in large kettle until crisp. Add diced onions and cook slowly until yellowed, not brown. Add potatoes and enough water so that potatoes are covered. Bring to a boil. Place fish (whole pieces) on top of potatoes. Add small, whole, peeled onion and seasonings. Cook slowly until potatoes are tender and fish is cooked through. Do not break up fish. Pour in both kinds of milk and heat through thoroughly. Do not boil. Chowder is best when cooked and left to stand (in refrigerator) for an hour or so. Reheat. Add butter and remove whole onion. Serve with crackers and pickles (pilot crackers and sour cucumber pickles are best). Serves 6.
Mrs. A.C. Archibald, *Eastport, Maine*

SEAFOOD CASSEROLE SUPREME

4 cups cooked brown rice
1 stick butter (¼ pound)
4 large mushrooms, sliced thin
3 large tomatoes, peeled and cut
   in wedges
¼ cup grated onion or
   1 tablespoon dried minced onion
2 cups cooked lobster or crab meat
   or 2 cans of either, rinsed
   and drained
½ teaspoon salt

2 or 3 dashes ground pepper
1 can water chestnuts, sliced
¼ cup slivered almonds
1 teaspoon monosodium glutamate
¼ teaspoon bitters
1 cup heavy cream
2 tablespoons minced parsley or
   1 tablespoon dried parsley
½ cup brandy
¼ pound cooked baby shrimp

Melt butter in large skillet. Add mushrooms; stir and cook for 5 minutes. Stir in tomatoes and onions. Cook for another 5 minutes. Add lobster (or crab), salt, pepper, water chestnuts, slivered almonds, monosodium glutamate and bitters. Stir and cook for 3 minutes. Stir in cream and cook until it bubbles. Add parsley and brandy and remove from heat. Line a 2-quart greased casserole with the cooked rice. Turn in the lobster or crab mixture. Top with the baby shrimp. Bake at 350° for 20 minutes. Serves 8.
Mel Wylie, *Richmond, California*

SCALLOPED OYSTERS

1 medium onion, chopped
½ cup chopped celery
1 clove garlic, chopped
¼ cup butter or margarine
2 cups toasted bread crumbs
1 quart oysters

1 teaspoon salt
1 teaspoon pepper
2 hard-cooked eggs, sliced
1 tablespoon Worcestershire sauce
1 pint milk

Cook onion, celery and garlic in small amount of butter until slightly brown; remove from pan. In baking dish, place a layer of bread crumbs, oysters, onion, celery, and garlic. Sprinkle salt and pepper over contents. Make a second layer of all ingredients, and top entire dish with sliced eggs. Add Worcestershire sauce to milk, and pour milk over entire dish. Place in oven at 325° for half hour, or until juice and milk are absorbed. Serves 10.

Mrs. Russell O. Behrens, *Apalachicola, Florida*

PERCH PIQUANT

2 (1-pound) boxes frozen perch
   (or similar fish)
2 large potatoes, peeled, cooked
   and sliced ¼ inch thick
½ pint sour cream

3 tablespoons prepared horseradish
½ cup mayonnaise
2 tablespoons pickle relish
1 teaspoon minced parsley
Salt and pepper to taste

Preheat oven to 350°. Lightly grease a shallow 2-quart casserole. Place fish and potatoes in casserole and dot sparingly with butter. Bake for 20 minutes. Mix sour cream, horseradish, mayonnaise, pickle relish, parsley, salt and pepper together and pour over fish and potatoes. Bake an additional 10 minutes. Serve while sauce is still bubbling. Serves 8.

Mrs. Beryl D. Ames, *New Orleans, Louisiana*

AHOY CASSEROLE

1 (8-ounce) package egg noodles
3 tablespoons butter or margarine
3 tablespoons flour
1½ cups milk
1 (11-ounce) can cream
   mushroom soup
1 (10-ounce) package frozen peas
1 cup grated cheese

½ teaspoon salt
¼ teaspoon pepper
1½ pounds scallops, fresh or frozen
   (thawed)
1 cup fresh mushrooms, sliced
¼ cup diced celery
2 tablespoons butter or margarine

Cook noodles as directed on package and drain. Melt 3 tablespoons butter in saucepan, stir in flour; add milk gradually, stirring constantly. After milk comes to a boil, blend in undiluted soup, frozen peas, ½ cup cheese and seasonings. Set aside. Sauté scallops, mushrooms and celery in 2 tablespoons butter. Drain and add to cheese sauce. Combine this mixture with noodles. Pour into greased casserole and top with remaining cheese. Bake at 400° for about 25 minutes. Serves 6 to 8.

Mary N. Walker, *Harbor City, California*

SHRIMP OR FISH CREOLE

2½ pounds shrimp (cooked) or fish
  (fresh or frozen tuna, etc.)
2 medium onions, choppsed
1 cup green pepper, finely chopped
1½ cups celery, cut in large pieces
¼ cup bacon drippings or oil
3 cans condensed tomato soup
  (10¾ ounces each)
1 tablespoon vinegar

1/8 teaspoon garlic powder
1 bay leaf
4 teaspoons chili powder
3 dashes Tabasco sauce
2 teaspoon salt
Dash Worcestershire sauce
Dash black pepper
½ to ¾ cup white wine

Sauté onion, green pepper and celery in oil until tender. Add remaining ingredients except fish; simmer 30 minutes. Add shrimp or fish and simmer for 10 to 15 minutes. Serve over hot rice. Serves 10.

David Savidge, *Fair Oaks, California*

DANISH SHRIMP SALAD

3 pounds shrimp, shelled
  and deveined
1 tablespoon shrimp spice
¾ cup mayonnaise
½ cup dairy sour cream
2 tablespoons minced onions
3 tablespoons lemon juice
2 to 3 tablespoons chopped

fresh dill
2 teaspoons salt
¼ teaspoon pepper
3 to 4 drops liquid hot
  pepper seasoning
Greens (romaine or Boston lettuce),
  washed

Cook the shrimp in water to cover with the shrimp spice, 5 to 8 minutes. Cool shrimp in the broth. Mix together mayonnaise, sour cream, onion, lemon juice, dill, salt, pepper and pepper seasoning. Drain shrimp and place in bowl; add dressing and mix well. Chill several hours. To serve, arrange shrimp on bed of greens. Serves 6.

Bess Slagle, *St. Peters, Missouri*

"What's for dinner?"

PARTY SHRIMP

2 pounds large shrimp
1 tablespoon lemon juice
3 tablespoons salad oil
¾ cup raw rice
2 tablespoons margarine
¼ cup minced green peppers
¼ cup minced onions

1 teaspoon salt
1/8 teaspoon pepper
1 can condensed tomato soup
1 cup heavy cream
½ cup sherry
½ cup slivered almonds

Cook shrimp in boiling salted water for 5 minutes. Place in 2-quart casserole. Sprinkle with lemon juice, oil. Meanwhile cook rice as package directs. Mix shrimp and rice and chill. Sauté peppers and onions in butter. Mix all ingredients in recipe together, with the exception of the almonds. Bake at 350° for 55 minutes. Top with slivered almonds. Serves 6.

Kay Conrad, *Wayland, Massachusetts*

SWEET-SOUR SHRIMP

1 medium onion, quartered
1 cup celery sliced diagonally
2 tablespoons salad oil
2/3 cup firmly packed brown sugar
2 tablespoons cornstarch
½ teaspoon salt
1/8 teaspoon ginger
1/3 cup vinegar

3 tablespoons soy sauce
1 (6-ounce) can pineapple juice
1¼ cups water
2 cups cubed pineapple
1 pound cooked shrimp
1 green pepper cut into
 1-inch pieces

Sauté onion and celery in hot oil until clear but not brown. Dissolve sugar, cornstarch, salt and ginger in vinegar and soy sauce. Add this mixture plus pineapple juice and water to the vegetables. Cook, stirring constantly until thickened. Add pineapple, shrimp and green pepper. Cover and cook for about 5 minutes. Serve over hot rice. Serves 4 to 6.

Helene Drown, *Rolling Hills, California*

SOLE AND CRAB

1 pint sour cream (2 cups)
3 egg yolks
3 tablespoons lemon juice
 (or white wine)

Salt and pepper
2 pounds filet of sole
1 or 2 packages (6-ounce) frozen crab

Mix sour cream, egg yolks, lemon juice, salt and pepper. Cover bottom of 9-by-13-inch baking dish with thin layer of sour cream mixture. Place layer of sole on sauce, season with salt and pepper. Cover with layer of crab, then second layer of sole. Cover with rest of sour cream mixture. Bake at 350° about 30 minutes or until sole flakes easily. Serves 6.

Mrs. C. N. Christensen, Indiana State Symphony Society, *Indianapolis, Indiana*

BREAD

In Time of Knead

SOUTHERN CORNBREAD
By Mary Alice Sharpe

Cornbread, like the polenta of northern Italy, is hearty, nutritious, cheap. In Italy, the cornmeal is poured slowly into salted boiling water until the water is saturated and a kind of wet cake is made which is served as a base for meatless stews and tomato sauces, and then fried the next morning with cheese for breakfast. In the South, the bread is cooked in the oven rather than on top of the stove and here the principle of overcook is deadly. It should be crusty on the outside of the pan and almost mushy in the center. And it should be eaten so hot butter doesn't stand a chance. Burnt fingers and a smile should be the only memory.

1½ cups white cornmeal	½ stick butter
½ cup self-rising flour	2 eggs, slightly beaten
2 tablespoons sugar	1½ cups buttermilk

Mix cornmeal, flour and sugar. Mix butter, eggs and buttermilk and stir into dry mixture. Bake in greased pan about 20 minutes in preheated 400 to 450° oven.

A piece of cornbread with a bowl of vegetable soup makes an unpretentious winter lunch, with stick-to-the-ribs-rather-than-some-other-area vitality.

HONEY BREAD

Homemade bread baked with honey instead of sugar will remain moist longer. The following recipe is for a fruit loaf that makes an excellent gift or a morning snack with coffee.

1¼ cups sifted all-purpose flour	1 cup buttermilk
1 teaspoon salt	3 tablespoons oil or shortening
½ teaspoon baking soda	2 eggs, well beaten
2 teaspoons baking powder	½ cup raisins or chopped dates
1 cup whole wheat flour	1 cup finely chopped
2/3 cup honey	walnuts or pecans

Sift the flour again with the salt, soda and baking powder. Add the whole wheat flour. Separately, mix the honey, buttermilk and oil with the beaten eggs. Stir in the dry ingredients. Do not over-stir. Fold in the nuts and the dates or raisins. Spoon the batter into a greased 9x5x3-inch loaf pan. Bake for 50 to 60 minutes in a 325° (moderate) oven.

Popovers are as light as milkweed blowing in the wind. They're easy to make and their mystery is in the two oven speeds (though there's no reason to tell anybody that).

2 eggs
1 cup milk
1 cup sifted all-purpose flour

½ teaspoon salt
1 tablespoon salad oil

Mix eggs in bowl with milk, flour and salt. Beat 1½ minutes with electric beater. Add salad oil and beat for ½ minute more. Don't overbeat. Fill 6 to 8 well-greased custard cups or a muffin pan about half full. Bake at 475° for 15 minutes. Reduce heat to 350° and bake 25 to 30 minutes, until browned. Before removing from the oven, prick each popover with a fork to let the steam out. You can stuff these with filling—meat, or cheese sauce, or a mushroom, parsley and almond mixture. By themselves, with butter or margarine, they're unforgettable.

ORANGE-DATE-NUT BREAD

The closer bread is to cake, the better. So say some. Children won't argue. And parents might not if the cake is an orange date nut loaf, full of natural ingredients, yet sweet enough to tempt little teeth away from cavity-making, jaw-breaking candies.

1 package pitted dates
  cut into small pieces
  (about 8 ounces)
2 tablespoons shortening
1 tablespoon grated or shredded
  orange peel
½ cup fresh orange juice
1 egg, beaten

2 cups sifted
  all-purpose flour
1/3 cup sugar
1 teaspoon soda
1 teaspoon baking powder
½ teaspoon salt
½ cup chopped pecans

Put the dates and shortening in a large bowl and pour ½ cup of boiling water over them. When this has cooled, add the orange juice and peeling. Stir in the egg. Sift together flour, baking powder, soda, salt, and sugar. Add to the mixture, stirring until just blended. Add the pecans. Pour into a greased, floured loaf pan, about 8 by 4 inches. Bake at 325° for about an hour. Before turning out of pan, cool for about 10 minutes. This may be stored in foil in the refrigerator.

WAFFLES A LA JOHNSON
By Nunally Johnson

Two cupfuls of flour are mixed in a sifter with two teaspoonfuls of baking powder, a half teaspoonful of baking soda and a pinch of salt. Beat this lovely conglomeration into a batter with milk, using the latter as needed for a fairly thick consistency. Add four tablespoonfuls of melted lard. Toss in an egg and continue to beat until the iron is good and hot.

At the end of five minutes one of the handsomest waffles you ever saw will emerge from this iron and, served with butter, will make another man out of you.

CINNAMON, RAISIN LOAF

1 package active dry yeast
¼ cup warm water
½ cup lukewarm milk
1 tablespoon sugar
1 teaspoon salt
1 egg
1 tablespoon margarine

1 tablespoon ground ginger
2 teaspoons grated lemon rind
2/3 cup raisins
2 2/3 to 3 cups unbleached flour
3 tablespoons margarine, melted
Cinnamon
Brown sugar

Dissolve yeast in water in large bowl, adding a pinch of sugar to prove yeast. Stir milk, sugar, salt, egg, margarine, ginger, lemon rind and half the flour into yeast mixture. Mix until smooth. Add raisins and enough flour to make handling easy. Turn onto floured board and knead in only as much of the remaining flour as will knead in easily. Place in greased bowl, turning so that top is also oiled. Cover and let rise until doubled.

Shape into 11-by-17-inch rectangle on very lightly floured board. Spread with melted margarine, shake on cinnamon and sprinkle lightly with brown sugar. Roll up and shape into loaf. Place in oiled pan and let rise, covered, until doubled. Before baking, brush top with melted margarine and sprinkle lightly with brown sugar. Bake at 425° for 25 to 30 minutes. If sugar becomes too brown, cover loaf with foil for remainder of cooking time. Yield: 1 loaf.

Mrs. Dee Stein, *Lincolnwood, Illinois*

66

"Good morning to you, good morning to you, good morning dear sweetheart, good morning to you."

ARNO'S BREAD

2 packages dry yeast
1/3 cup lukewarm water
2 tablespoons sugar
12 cups unbleached all-purpose
  flour
2 cups milk
2 medium potatoes
  (peeled, boiled and mashed)
2 cups potato water
  (from potatoes above)

3 tablespoons melted shortening
1 tablespoon salt
1 cup pitted dates
½ cup dry apricots
½ cup pitted prunes
1 cup raisins
½ pound margarine, soft
1 cup brown sugar
1 tablespoon cinnamon
1 small jar honey

Dissolve yeast in warm water with 2 tablespoons sugar. Let stand a few minutes. Place 6 cups flour in large mixing bowl. Add yeast mixture, milk, mashed potatoes and potato water. Mix with spoon until batter is soft and bubbly. Cover with dish towel and let rise in warm place until doubled in bulk (about 1 hour).

Add remaining 6 cups of flour, melted shortening and salt. Chop dates, apricots and prunes and add to batter along with raisins. Place dough on floured board and knead for 10 minutes. Place in mixing bowl, cover and let rise again for 1 hour.

Punch down dough and divide into 4 equal parts. Roll each part into a 12-by-16-inch rectangle. Spread with soft margarine and sprinkle with mixture of brown sugar and cinnamon. Drip on honey in a crisscross pattern. Roll up dough, tuck in ends and place in greased bread pans. Cover pans with towel and let rise to top of pans (at least one hour). Bake in preheated 400° oven on middle rack 10 minutes. Reduce heat to 350° and bake 50 minutes longer. Remove bread from oven and turn out of pans onto cooling racks. Wait 20 minutes before cutting. Yield: 4 loaves.

A. R. and Polly Justman, *Fort Walton Beach, Florida*

NO-KNEAD
GRANOLA SWEET BREAD

1 quart skimmed milk
1½ cups shortening
3 tablespoons salt
6 eggs
1 cup sugar

3 packages active dry yeast
2 cups granola
2 cups raisins
Flour

Heat milk, shortening and salt on medium burner until shortening melts. Cool slightly. Beat eggs and sugar together in large bowl. Add milk and shortening mixture to eggs, then yeast, granola and raisins. Add flour until dough is slightly thicker than cake batter but thin enough to pour into well-greased bread pans. Fill pans to half full. Using warm setting on oven (not more than 150°), allow bread to rise in oven for 45 minutes. Raise temperature setting to 275° and bake slowly for another 45 minutes or until done. Glaze with powdered sugar thinned with hot water. Cool before slicing. Yield: 5 loaves.

Fran Gorton, *Spokane, Washington*

CONVERTIBLE EVERY DAY WHITE BREAD

9 to 10 cups all-purpose flour, sifted
3 tablespoons sugar
1 tablespoon salt
2 cups very hot water

2 cups cold water
3 packages dry yeast
½ cup vegetable shortening
  or cooking oil

Use glass bread pans or equally heavy material. Place all flour in large bowl. With wooden spoon, press flour up around sides of bowl, leaving a hole or depression in middle of flour.

In a smaller bowl, stir together the sugar, 3 tablespoons flour (taken from large bowl) and salt. Add very hot water and stir smooth. Add cold water and stir smooth. Then add the 3 packages of yeast. Stir, cover and keep warm for about 15 to 20 minutes, until mixture is light and bubbly. Stir and then dump yeast mixture (all at once) into the depression of flour in large bowl. Stirring slowly from bottom, add flour until a soft batter is made. Beat this until it seems smooth, being careful not to use too much flour at this stage. Cover and keep warm for 15 to 20 minutes. Then stir slowly from bottom, adding a bit of flour constantly until you can use your hands to knead all remaining flour, and dough becomes soft and spongy. Place on board and continue kneading until dough does not stick to your hands, about 5 minutes. Grease large bowl and put dough back in bowl. Grease dough and cover. Keep in warm place until doubled in bulk.

Punch down and knead again until soft. Grease and let rise again in bowl until doubled. Always knead on floured board. Punch down again and knead for a few minutes before forming into 3 loaves. Place in well-greased pans and "bathe" loaves with melted shortening. Let rise until doubled, keeping warm. Handle carefully while placing in a preheated oven of 425°. Bake for 30 or 35 minutes. Check after first 15 minutes. If it seems a bit hot, turn back to 375° or 400°. When done, remove from pans and cool on rack. These loaves may be frozen and kept for an indefinite time in freezer. Yield: 3 loaves.

Mrs. Tod S. Chearonn, *Londonville, Ohio*

GRANDMA VOELKER'S COFFEE CAKE

1 cake yeast
1 cup lukewarm water
½ cup lard
1 cup boiling water
1 cup cold water

½ cup sugar
2 to 3 eggs, beaten
1½ teaspoons salt
9 cups flour
  (approximate)

Soak yeast in 1 cup lukewarm water and set aside. Melt lard in 1 cup boiling water. Add cold water, sugar, eggs, salt and yeast to lard mixture. Stir in about 4 cups of flour and beat 3 minutes (as for cake). Work in the remaining flour and keep beating until you have a soft dough. Place in greased bowl and let rise until doubled in bulk. (May be regrigerated overnight, or longer.) Divide dough and place in four 8-inch or 9-inch round cake pans. Brush with melted butter or margarine and sprinkle with a mixture of sugar and cinnamon. Let rise again until doubled. Bake in 350° to 375° oven for 20 to 30 minutes. Yield: 4 coffee cakes.

Mrs. Adolph Voelker, *Tell City, Indiana*

ALMOND ROSE ROLLS

1 package active dry yeast
¼ cup lukewarm water
1/8 cup margarine
1/8 cup vegetable shortening
¼ cup sugar
1 teaspoon salt
1 tablespoon grated lime rind
½ cup scalded milk
½ cup ice water

1 egg, slightly beaten
4 cups presifted all-purpose flour
1/3 cup squeeze liquid margarine
3/4 cup firmly packed
  light brown sugar
2 tablespoons instantized flour
1 teaspoon almond flavoring
1 teaspoon rose extract
Cream

Dissolve yeast in lukewarm water. Combine margarine, shortening, sugar, salt, grated lime rind and scalded milk. Add ice water; cool to lukewarm. Blend in egg and the dissolved yeast. Add flour gradually, mixing well after each addition. Cover and let rise in warm place 45 to 60 minutes.

Combine squeeze liquid margarine, brown sugar, instantized flour, almond and rose extracts and mix well. Reserve as filling for rolls.

Roll dough into two 12-by-10-inch rectangles. Spread with almond rose filling. Roll as for jelly roll and cut into ½ inch slices. Arrange slices on greased baking sheet. Flatten to ¼-inch thickness. Place a blanched almond and preserved rose petals (if available) in center of each roll. Let rise 30 to 45 minutes. Brush tops of rolls lightly with cream. Bake in preheated 400° oven 12 to 15 minutes. Remove immediately from baking sheet. Yield: 2½ dozen.

Mrs. Helen Mize, *High Point, North Carolina*

BUTTERSCOTCH PARTY ROLLS

1 cup evaporated milk
1 cup brown sugar
½ cup butter
1 tablespoon vanilla
4 eggs
2 teaspoons salt

2 packages active dry yeast
½ cup lukewarm water
6 cups white flour
1 cup chopped nuts
2 cups confectioners' sugar

Combine evaporated milk and brown sugar in a saucepan and cook for 5 minutes after mixture has started to boil, stirring constantly. Take off stove and stir in butter and vanilla. Reserve ½ cup of this butterscotch sauce for the filling and frosting. Break eggs into a large mixing bowl and beat well. Add salt, lukewarm butterscotch sauce, and yeast that has been dissolved in the lukewarm water. Add 3 cups flour. Mix together using low speed, then beat at medium speed for 3 minutes. Stir in the remaining flour and half the nuts. Scrape bowl down, cover, and let rise until double in bulk. To the ½ cup reserved butterscotch sauce stir in 2 cups sifted confectioners' sugar.

When the dough is doubled in size, punch down and roll out to an 18-by-24-inch rectangle. Spread half the filling on the dough. Roll up as for jelly roll, starting with the 24-inch side. Cut in 36 equal pieces. Put in greased muffin tins and top each roll with an equal amount of the remaining filling and nuts. Let rise until double in size. Bake at 375° for 20 minutes, or until golden brown. Yield: 36 rolls.

Marilee Jean Johnson, *Robbinsdale, Minnesota*

FRUIT MUFFINS

1 cake compressed yeast
¼ cup lukewarm water
½ cup old-fashioned oatmeal
½ cup yellow cornmeal
½ cup All Bran
½ cup brown sugar

1 teaspoon salt
1 rounded tablespoon shortening
2 cups boiling water
5 cups white flour
Cooked prunes

Dissolve yeast in lukewarm water. Mix together oatmeal, cornmeal, All Bran, brown sugar, salt and shortening in bowl. Pour on boiling water and let stand until lukewarm. Add yeast mixture and beat a few minutes with spoon. Add 5 cups white flour and knead into soft ball.

Place in greased bowl and let rise until doubled in bulk. Spoon into large muffin pans, filling half full. Make deep hole in center of each muffin and place cooked prune deep in hole. Lightly spread muffin dough with butter and let rise again until doubled. Bake in 350° oven approximately 25 minutes or until golden brown on top. Remove from pans, spread tops with butter and sprinkle with wheat germ.

Mary E. Ralph, *Forsyth, Missouri*

SOUR CREAM NUT-FILLED ROLLS

4 cups sifted flour
¼ cup sugar
1½ teaspoons salt
1 cup (2 sticks) margarine
2 yeast cakes or packages of

dry yeast
2 tablespoons sugar
½ cup milk
1 cup sour cream
2 beaten eggs

Cut the margarine into dry ingredients in large bowl, as for pie crust. Make a "well" in center of mixture. Dissolve yeast and sugar in milk. Place in "well" with sour cream and eggs. Stir all ingredients together, using a large spoon to mix, forming a soft dough. Cover with a damp cloth or merely sift a little flour over the top of dough and place bowl of dough in refrigerator to rise overnight. The next morning, roll out half of dough at a time on well-floured board, forming a circle. Cut 12 pie-shaped wedges from each circle. Put a spoonful of nut filling at wide end of each wedge. Roll up, sealing ends as you start by pulling ends of dough up over the nut mixture, then rolling toward point of dough. Let rise in 2 greased 9-by-12-by-2-inch pans, or use two jelly-roll pans, if preferred. When rolls have doubled in size, bake at 350° for 20 to 25 minutes. Soon after taking from the oven, drizzle top with glaze.

Nut Filling:
¾ cup (1 stick) margarine
2 cups walnuts, ground

½ cup sugar
½ teaspoon cinnamon (optional)

Melt margarine in saucepan and add remaining ingredients.

Glaze:
¾ cup confectioners' sugar
1½ tablespoons water
½ teaspoon vanilla

Stir these 3 ingredients together in cup or bowl and drip over the rolls while they are still very warm from the oven.

Joyce H. Orcutt, *Punta Gorda, Florida*

DESSERTS

Executive Sweet

CREPES SUZETTES
By George Rector

I suppose that the famous crêpes Suzette are the culminating outburst of what the continent of Europe can do with a pancake. They do call for quite an array of liqueur bottles, but that's not so much of a handicap for the American cook as it was a short time ago, so here goes. Follow my lead and you'll have a stranglehold on one of the most eminent dishes in the world, and one that really deserves its reputation.

You want fairly substantial cakes here, so the eggs take a back seat. The formula for the batter is half a cup of flour, a tablespoon of sugar and a quarter teaspoon of salt, into which go half a cup of milk and one egg, to be stirred coonily until the batter is smooth. Get down the little frying pan—a little more than five inches is the right diameter—butter it well and, when it's hot, pour in just enough batter to cover the bottom when you turn it this way and that. Brown each cake nicely on both sides and stack them in a warm place while you fix the sauce—a process which will fill the kitchen with the odors of paradise, although not the teetotal Mohammedan kind.

Beforehand you've rubbed eight lumps of sugar on the rinds of a lemon and an orange until the sugar is full of the oils—not so difficult as it sounds, although it takes time. Now you can break out the chafing dish that came with the wedding presents and melt a tablespoon of butter in it, adding four lumps of sugar to melt with the butter. Then in go a couple of tablespoons of rum or brandy, ditto of curaçao or Grand Marnier, ditto of benedictine. While that mixture of good things is getting good and hot, you fold four of your pancakes in quarters and then, when the sauce is hot as blazes, drop them in and sort of flop and fiddle with them—toss is the professional word—until they absorb all the sauce. You'll probably be dizzy from the smell, but carry on—repeat the sauce, toss the rest of the pancakes—the above recipe ought to make eight—and then you can sit down and discover what a swell cook you are.

SUITE TOOTH
By Mary Alice Sharpe

To really set the world on fire—or the reverse, which seems to be more what's wanted these days—serve this with hand-cranked honey ice cream.

In a saucepan, mix 1 quart milk, 1 quart heavy cream, 1¾ cups honey. Heat until lukewarm. (Be careful not to scorch.) Chill. Add 1 tablespoon of vanilla. Beat six egg whites until stiff. Using the same beater, beat the egg yolks until thick. Fold into the chilled mixture. Fill chilled freezer container 2/3 full with mixture, adding milk if necessary. Cover tightly, set in freezer tub and follow directions for right amounts of cracked ice and ice cream freezer salt. When mixture is frozen, remove dasher. Pack down ice cream. Replace cover. Return to freezer tub. Set in ice until ready to serve. Makes 1 gallon. To make chocolate, melt 2 cups of chocolate chips in the combination of warm milk and cream.

Since children will eat candy, you might try chocolate-nut squares made by melting a 6-ounce package of semisweet chocolate pieces in 3 tablespoons of honey and 1 teaspoon of vanilla over very low heat; stir just until the chocolate is smooth. Add a cup of coarsely chopped pecans or walnuts and ¼ teaspoon of salt. Pat candy into a buttered pan. When cool, cut into squares.

CAN'T WAIT APPLE CAKE

4 cups apples, diced
½ cup cooking oil
2 cups sugar
2 eggs, well beaten
2 cups flour

1½ teaspoons soda
½ teaspoon salt
1 teaspoon cinnamon
1 teaspoon vanilla
1 cup chopped walnuts

Combine apples, oil and sugar. Add beaten eggs. Sift together flour, soda, salt and cinnamon and add to batter. Stir in vanilla and nuts. Bake in greased 9-by-13-inch pan in 375° oven for about 45 minutes.

Lillian Freedman, *Van Nuys, California*

AUNT BERTHA SANBORN'S BLUEBERRY CAKE

1 3/4 cups flour
2 tablespoons baking powder
Pinch salt
1 cup sugar

¼ cup shortening or butter
1 egg, beaten
3/4 cup milk
1 cup or more floured berries

Sift together flour, baking powder and salt and set aside. Cream together sugar and shortening. Add egg and milk and beat well. Add sifted dry ingredients. Fold floured berries into the batter before the dry ingredients are completely moist and put in greased and lightly floured 9-by-5-inch loaf pan. Bake in preheated 350° oven 40 to 45 minutes or until top is golden brown. Serves 8.

Miss Lynne Ellen Zalesak, *Harwich Port, Massachusetts*

"Now, that's what I call a rum cake."

MAPLE BLUEBERRY CAKE
WITH LEMON GLAZE

¼ cup shortening
½ cup maple syrup
½ cup brown sugar
3/4 cup sour cream
2 eggs, beaten
3/4 cup blueberries, drained

2 cups flour
1 teaspoon ginger
1 teaspoon baking soda
¼ teaspoon salt
½ cup drained blueberry juice

Heat shortening, syrup, and sugar together in a saucepan. Add sour cream, beaten eggs, and blueberries. Sift dry ingredients, and add to batter. Mix well, and pour in greased 10-inch spring-form pan, or 10-inch bundt pan. Bake in 350° oven for 30 minutes, or until inserted knife comes out dry. After cake cools, pour reserved blueberry juice over the cake (this allows for the cake to become extra moist, before applying the lemon glaze).

Lemon Glaze:

1 tablespoon milk
2 tablespoons lemon juice
¾ cup confectioners' sugar

Gradually blend milk and lemon juice into confectioners' sugar and pour over cake before serving, let glaze set; then slice cake. Serves 10 to 12.
Mrs. Martha Swanson, *Killingworth, Connecticut*

HOLIDAY APPLE CAKE

3 cups chopped peeled baking apples
3/4 cup sugar
3/4 cup golden raisins
1/3 cup chopped almonds
3 tablespoons flour
1 teaspoon cinnamon
2½ cups unsifted flour
2 teaspoons baking powder

1½ teaspoons salt
2 eggs
1/3 cup oil
1/3 cup water
1/3 cup sugar
1½ teaspoons vanilla
Confectioners' sugar frosting

Combine chopped apples, 3/4 cup sugar, raisins, chopped nuts, 3 tablespoons flour and cinnamon. Set aside. Blend the flour, baking powder and salt. Beat together eggs, oil, water, 1/3 cup sugar and vanilla. Gradually stir in flour mixture until completely blended. Turn batter out onto well-floured board; with floured hands shape batter into ball and divide into 3 equal pieces. Roll out one piece to make a 9-inch square. Place it in an oiled 9-inch square baking pan. Cover with half of the apple mixture. Roll out the second piece just as the first piece and place over the apple layer; then cover with remaining apple mixture. Roll out third piece of dough also to 9-inch square and place over second apple layer to form top crust. Make several slits in it to allow the steam to escape. Bake in 350° oven 60 to 70 minutes. While warm frost with confectioners' sugar frosting. Frosting: Mix 1 cup confectioners' sugar with 2 tablespoons milk or water and ¼ teaspoon vanilla extract. Spread on warm cake. Serves 9.
Mrs. E. Duncan, *New Britain, Connecticut*

CARIN' ABOUTCHA CARROT CAKE

2 cups flour
2 teaspoons baking powder
1 teaspoon salt
1½ teaspoons soda
2 teaspoons cinnamon
2 cups sugar

1½ cups oil
4 eggs
2 cups grated carrots
1 (8½-ounce) can crushed pineapple
½ cup chopped nuts

Combine flour, baking powder, salt, soda and cinnamon. Add sugar, oil and eggs. Mix well. Add carrots, drained pineapple and nuts. Bake in 9-by-13-inch greased and floured pan at 350° for 35 to 40 minutes.

Frosting: (Optional)

½ cup butter
1 (8-ounce) package cream cheese
1 teaspoon vanilla

1 pound powdered sugar
Milk

Cream butter, cream cheese and vanilla. Add powdered sugar. If too thick, add milk to spreading consistency. Serves 12.

Lee Craig Douglas, *Los Angeles, California*

AUNT DOROTHY'S CHEESECAKE

13 graham crackers
3 tablespoons butter
1 pound cream cheese

1 cup sugar
3 eggs
1 teaspoon vanilla

Topping

1 pint sour cream
1 tablespoon sugar
½ teaspoon vanilla

Crush graham crackers; combine with butter and line an 8-by-12-inch or an 8-by-8-inch baking dish. Blend cream cheese, sugar, eggs and vanilla. Pour mixture in lining and bake 25 to 35 minutes in 350° preheated oven. Mix sour cream with 1 tablespoon sugar and ½ teaspoon vanilla. Spread this topping on cake after it has cooled. Place in oven at 300° for 5 minutes. Refrigerate overnight.

Mrs. Harry S. Gill, *South Yarmouth, Massachusetts*

CREAM CAKE

4 eggs, separated
1½ cups sugar
½ pint heavy cream

1 teaspoon vanilla
1¾ cups (self-rising)
   cake flour

Beat egg yolks until lemon colored. Add sugar and beat until well combined. Add cream and vanilla and blend at low speed. Add cake flour and mix thoroughly. Beat egg whites until stiff and fold into batter. Pour into greased 9-inch or 10-inch tube pan. Bake in 350° oven for approximately 1 hour.

Mrs. Donald S. Law, *Bradenton, Florida*

FROZEN MINT JULEP PIE

1 1/3 cups crushed zwieback or
   chocolate wafer crumbs
2 tablespoons sugar
¼ cup melted butter
1 envelope unflavored gelatin
½ cup sugar

1/8 teaspoon salt
3 eggs, separated
1 cup light cream
¼ cup bourbon
2 tablespoons mint-flavored jelly
1 cup heavy cream, whipped

Combine crumbs, 2 tablespoons sugar and melted butter. Butter a 10-inch pie plate and press crumbs firmly into the bottom and against sides of pan. Chill.

Combine gelatin, ¼ cup sugar, and salt in medium saucepan. Beat egg yolks lightly and add with light cream and bourbon to gelatin mixture. Cook over low heat, stirring constantly until custard coats the spoon. Stir in mint jelly. Chill until mixture begins to thicken. Beat egg whites to soft peaks. Gradually beat in remaining ¼ cup sugar; beat until meringue is stiff. Fold meringue and whipped cream into the thickened custard. Turn into crumb crust. Place in freezer until firm. To serve: remove to refrigerator shelf 2 hours before cutting. Garnish with sprigs of fresh mint. Makes 8 to 10 servings.

Bess Slagle, *St. Peters, Missouri*

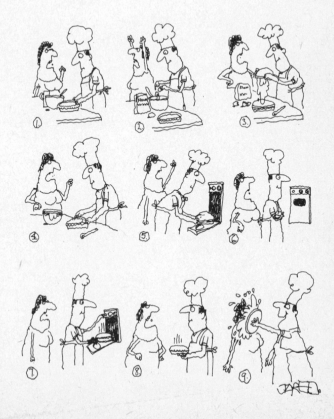

CHOICE PUMPKIN PIE

1 8-inch pie crust
1 tablespoon butter
1 cup rich milk, scalded
2 large eggs, beaten slightly
2/3 cup white sugar

¼ teaspoon salt
¼ teaspoon ginger
1/3 teaspoon mace
½ teaspoon cinnamon
1 cup light golden pumpkin

Add butter to scalded milk. Mix beaten eggs with sugar. Add salt, ginger, mace and cinnamon to pumpkin and add to egg mixture. Gradually add milk, beating gently just until mixed (not foamy). Pour into unbaked pie crust and bake in preheated 450° oven about 10 to 12 minutes to set crust. Then lower heat to 400° for about 5 minutes. As crust begins to turn a delicate brown on edges, lower heat to about 300° (filling must never start to bubble; if it should, you may have to lower heat to about 275°). Bake until a knife blade inserted in the center of the pie comes out clean. If baked properly, the entire crust should be a light golden brown on the bottom. Serve with butterscotch whipped cream below.

Butterscotch Sauce

1¼ cups brown sugar
2/3 cup dark corn syrup
4 tablespoons butter
3/4 cup thin cream

1 pint heavy cream, whipped
1 teaspoon vanilla
1 teaspoon rum flavoring

Mix brown sugar, syrup and butter in pan and bring to a boil, stirring constantly until syrup forms a very soft ball in cold water. Remove from heat and immediately pour in 3/4 cup thin cream. Beat cream into the syrup until thoroughly mixed. Pour into jars, leaving a 2-inch space at the top for mixing the sauce each time before it is served. Cover; refrigerate. This sauce keeps indefinitely under refrigeration. For a double recipe of the pie, whip 1 pint of cream until just stiff. Fold in ½ cup of the butterscotch sauce; add 1 teaspoon vanilla and 1 teaspoon rum flavoring. Serve on top of each slice of pie.

Crust for Pumpkin Pie

3 cups flour
½ teaspoon salt
1 cup lard

1/3 cup vinegar
1/3 cup cold water

Mix flour with salt. Cut in lard until like fine meal. Mix vinegar and cold water and add to flour mixture. Mix until dough will leave the bowl in a clean ball. Wrap in plastic wrap and put in plastic bag. Seal tightly and refrigerate. Makes 2 medium-size double crust pies. Remove from refrigerator an hour or two before using.

Ruth G. Gleason, *Helena, Montana*

RAISIN-BLACK WALNUT PIE

1 unbaked 8-inch pie shell
4 eggs, beaten
½ cup brown sugar, packed
½ cup white sugar

¼ cup soft butter or margarine
1½ cups light corn syrup
1 cup black walnuts
1 cup chopped raisins

Combine eggs, sugar, butter and beat until thick and fluffy. Add syrup and beat well. Fold in nutmeats and raisins. Stir gently. Turn into unbaked pie shell and bake in 375° preheated oven for 40 to 50 minutes or until center is firm. Serve plain or topped with ice cream or whipped cream. Serves 6.

Mrs. Lyle H. Camp, *Fullerton, California*

EGGNOG PIE

1 baked 9-inch pastry shell
1½ teaspoons unflavored gelatin
2 tablespoons cold water
3 egg yolks
2/3 cup sugar
1/8 teaspoon salt

1 teaspoon vanilla
2 tablespoons milk
3 egg whites
½ cup heavy cream, whipped
2 to 4 tablespoons rum (optional)
1 teaspoon nutmeg

Soak gelatin in cold water. Beat egg yolks, add 1/3 cup of sugar, salt, vanilla, and milk. Cook over very low heat until thickened. Add gelatin to hot custard mixture. Stir until completely dissolved. Beat egg whites until stiff but not dry; gradually beat in other 1/3 cup of sugar. Fold the custard mixture into the egg whites. Set aside to cool. Fold in whipped cream and rum. Pour into baked pastry shell. Sprinkle top with nutmeg and place in refrigerator until firm. Serves 6 to 8.

Mrs. Frank C. Volpert, *Peru, Indiana*

GRAND FINALE PIE

1 baked 9-inch pastry shell
2 egg whites
1 cup sugar
2 tablespoons water
¼ teaspoon cream of tartar
¼ teaspoon salt

½ cup chocolate chips
1 cup coconut
1 cup chopped nuts
1 teaspoon vanilla
2 cups whipped cream
  or whipped topping

Combine in the top of a double boiler the first five ingredients. Beat with an electric mixer over boiling water for 5 minutes until the mixture stands in stiff peaks. Remove from hot water; add chocolate chips. Let stand about 10 minutes to melt. Fold coconut, nuts and vanilla into the cooked mixture. Cool, then fold in whipped cream. Gently pile into baked pastry shell. Refrigerate for an hour or longer. Serves 6 to 8.

Marleen Carol Johnson, *Robbinsdale, Minnesota*

AFTER DINNER COCKTAIL PIE

Vanilla Wafer Crumb Crust

1½ cups crushed vanilla wafers
1/3 cup melted butter or margarine

Mix vanilla wafer crumbs and melted butter well. Press mixture into bottom and around sides of a 9-inch pie plate. Bake in preheated 375° oven for 8 minutes. Cool.

Cocktail Chiffon Filling

2¾ teaspoons unflavored gelatin
  (little less than 1 package)
¼ cup cold water
¼ cup egg yolks (about 4 large)
5/8 cup sugar
¼ teaspoon salt

1/3 cup fresh lime juice
3 drops green food coloring
1/3 cup light rum
5/8 cup egg whites at room
  temperature (about 4 large)
¼ cup sugar

Soften gelatin in cold water. Beat egg yolks with 5/8 cup sugar and salt until light in top of double boiler. Add lime juice gradually. Cook over boiling water, stirring constantly, until mixture thickens slightly—about 3 to 4 minutes. Do not over cook! Remove from heat. Add softened gelatin and stir in thoroughly. Add food coloring and rum. Chill in refrigerator until mixture thickens—20 to 25 minutes. Beat egg whites until foamy throughout; gradually add remaining ¼ cup sugar and continue to beat until they hold shape in distinct folds. Gently fold the cooled lime-rum mixture into the egg whites. Pour into cooled Vanilla Wafer Crust and chill.

Whipped Cream Topping

1 cup heavy cream
2 tablespoons sugar
½ teaspoon vanilla extract

Combine heavy cream, sugar, and vanilla. Whip until soft peaks form. Spread on pie and decorate with finely grated lime rind.

Donald L. Herman, *Yardley, Pennsylvania*

HELEN'S LEMON PIE

1 baked 8-inch pie shell
1½ cups sugar
3 tablespoons cornstarch
1 tablespoon flour
Pinch of salt

Grated rind and juice of
  1½ lemons
1½ cups water
3 eggs, separated
3 teaspoons sugar

Combine sugar, cornstarch, flour and salt. Add grated lemon rind and juice, water and egg yolks. Cook until thick in double boiler and pour into baked pie shell. Beat egg whites. Gradually add 3 teaspoons sugar and beat until snowy white and stiff. Spread on top of pie. Bake at 350° for 15 minutes to brown. Serves 6.

Mrs. Helen L. Mayo, *Benton, Illinois*

GOLDEN NUGGET DISCOVERY PIE

Pastry:

1¼ cups all-purpose flour
½ teaspoon salt
½ cup shortening

3 tablespoons instant cocoa
3 tablespoons boiling water

Filling:

1/3 cup sugar
1 (8-ounce) package cream cheese
2 tablespoons milk
2 unbeaten eggs

1 tablespoon grated orange rind
1 teaspoon vanilla
½ cup (2 medium) orange sections,
  cut into small pieces

Prepare pastry: Combine the flour and salt. Measure the shortening, instant cocoa and water into mixing bowl; mix well. Add dry ingredients all at once. Stir quickly until mixture holds together. Form into a ball. Flatten to ½-inch thickness. Roll out between lightly floured waxed paper to a circle 1½ inches larger than an inverted 8-inch pie pan. Fit loosely into pan; prick with fork. Fold edge to form rim; flute. Bake at 425° for 12 to 15 minutes.

Prepare orange cheese filling: Cream the sugar and cream cheese with the milk. Add eggs, one at a time, beating well after each. Blend in orange rind and vanilla. Fold in orange sections. Pour into baked shell. Bake at 350° for 20 to 25 minutes, until center is almost firm. Chill. If desired, top with Orange Whipped Cream and sprinkle with chopped toasted almonds about 1 hour before serving. Chill. Serves 6 to 8.

Orange Whipped Cream: Beat 1 cup whipping cream until thick. Stir in 2 tablespoons sugar and 2 tablespoons grated orange rind.

Mrs. Harold Johnston *Anaheim, California*

HARVEY WALLBANGER PIE

22 chocolate wafers rolled fine
4 tablespoons melted butter

Mix wafers and butter together. Pat into a 9-inch greased pie pan covering bottom and sides. Bake 8 minutes. Cool.

22 marshmallows
3/4 cup orange juice
1 tablespoon Cointreau

3 tablespoons Galliano
½ teaspoon grated orange rind
1 pint whipped cream

Melt marshmallows with orange juice in top of double boiler over boiling water. Cool. Add Galliano, Cointreau, and grated orange rind. Refrigerate until slightly thickened. Fold in half of whipped cream. Pour into crust. Refrigerate until firm. Garnish with remaining whipped cream.

Marjorie V. Anderson, *Mount Zion, Illinois*

BRANDIED CHERRY BUTTER BALLS

Cookie Dough

2/3 cup granulated white sugar
½ teaspoon double-acting
  baking powder
¼ teaspoon salt
½ cup butter or

margarine (softened)
1 large unbeaten egg
1 teaspoon imitation brandy extract
1¾ cups pre-sifted all-purpose flour

Brandied Cherry Filling

30 maraschino cherries
  (drained on paper toweling)
1 tablespoon pure honey

1 teaspoon imitation brandy extract
3 tablespoons walnuts, chopped

Glaze

1 cup unsifted confectioners' sugar
1 tablespoon light corn syrup
2 tablespoons maraschino cherry juice

(heated until hot)
½ teaspoon imitation brandy extract

Prepare brandied cherry filling by placing cherries close together on wax paper. Combine honey and brandy and brush tops of cherries with this combination using a pastry brush. Sprinkle cherries with walnuts. Set aside.

Make cookie dough by combining all ingredients except flour in a large mixing bowl and beat at low speed for 1 minute. Gradually add the flour at low speed until a stiff dough forms (about 1 minute). Form dough into a large ball. Pinch small balls of dough (1 well-rounded teaspoonful) from prepared dough; flatten with fingers in palm of hand to about 1/8-inch thickness. Place 1 brandied cherry with honey and nuts on it in center of dough. Roll to form a ball. Repeat with remaining dough and cherries. Place each ball on an ungreased cookie sheet about 2 inches apart and bake on second and third oven racks from bottom of preheated 350° oven for 12 to 15 minutes, until cookies are delicately golden color.

When cookies are cool, make glaze and spread about ½ teaspoonful on top and sides of each cookie using the inside of teaspoon to spread glaze. Place on wax paper until glaze sets. Yield: 2½ dozen.

Mrs. Gloria Dutrumble, *Uncasville, Connecticut*

HONEY BARS

½ cup shortening
½ cup sugar
½ cup honey
1 egg, well beaten
2/3 cup sifted flour
½ teaspoon baking soda

½ teaspoon baking powder
¼ teaspoon salt
1 cup quick-cooking rolled oats
1 cup flaked coconut
1 teaspoon vanilla
½ cup chopped nuts

Cream shortening, sugar and honey until light and fluffy. Add egg and blend. Sift flour with soda, baking powder and salt; add to creamed mixture. Add oats, coconut, vanilla and nuts. Spread in greased 10½-by-15-inch pan; bake in 350° oven for 20 to 25 minutes. When cool, cut into bars. Yield: 36 bars.

Madelyn E. Jones, *Waterbury, Connecticut*

BUTTERSCOTCH COOKIES

½ cup margarine or butter
1½ cups light brown sugar,
  packed in cup
2 eggs
2½ cups all-purpose flour
½ teaspoon double-action

baking powder
1 teaspoon soda
½ teaspoon salt
1 cup sour cream
1 teaspoon vanilla
½ cup nuts (optional)

Cream margarine and sugar. Add eggs and beat. Sift flour, baking powder, soda and salt together and add alternately to batter with the sour cream to which vanilla has been added. Stir in nuts and chill until dough is firm. Drop by teaspoons 2 inches apart on lightly greased baking sheet. Bake 10 to 15 minutes in moderate hot oven (about 400°.)

Brown Butter Icing

1/3 cup butter
1½ cups sifted confectioners' sugar

1 teaspoon vanilla
1 to 2 tablespoons hot water

Melt butter over low heat until golden brown. Blend in confectioners' sugar and vanilla. Stir in slowly 1 to 2 tablespoons hot water until of consistency to spread.

Kathleen Wagner, *Peru, Indiana*

"Would you mind repeating that recipe—without the arsenic?"

ALMOND CUSTARD

1 cup almonds, grated or ground
3 eggs
¼ cup sugar

1/8 teaspoon salt
2 cups milk, scalded
1 teaspoon almond flavoring

Sprinkle bottoms of 5 custard cups with half of the almonds and press down. Beat eggs until light. Add sugar and salt. Stir scalded milk into egg mixture. Add almond flavoring and pour into cups. Sprinkle the remaining almonds on top. Bake in 350° oven 40 to 45 minutes. Serves 5.

Mrs. Deveaux M. Ackley, *Jackson, Mississippi*

CRESCENT APPLE DESSERT

1 package refrigerated crescent rolls
4 tablespoons soft butter
1/8 cup cinnamon-sugar mix
2 cups warm applesauce

1½ teaspoons cinnamon
½ cup sour cream
  (or sweet whipped cream)

Open rolls, attach 2 triangles, making a square. Place on cookie sheet. Repeat with other roll. Butter tops and sprinkle with cinnamon-sugar mix. Bake in 350° oven for 10 minutes. Split and butter bottoms. Alternate pastry and applesauce (flavored with cinnamon). End with sugared top. Spread with sour cream or sweet whipped cream. Serve warm. Cut servings with a knife and serve with a spoon. Serves 4.

Mrs. Carl L. Johnson, *Pompton Plains, New Jersey*

APPLE-RAISIN-NUT PUDDING

2 cups chopped tart apples
½ cup raisins
1 cup chopped nut meats,
  preferably pecans
1 cup sugar
¼ cup vegetable shortening
1 egg, large

1 cup flour
1 teaspoon baking powder
1 teaspoon soda
1 teaspoon cinnamon
¼ teaspoon nutmeg
¼ teaspoon salt

Topping

2 tablespoons melted butter
5 tablespoons brown sugar
2 tablespoons cream

Wash, quarter and core unpeeled apples. Run apples through food chopper and measure. Run raisins and nut meats through food chopper. Cream sugar and shortening; add egg and beat until waxy. Sift dry ingredients into creamed mixture; batter will be stiff, the only liquid being the chopped apples. Add chopped apples, raisins and nuts to batter. Beat until well mixed. Pour into 9-by-13-inch shallow pan (greased). Bake about 40 minutes in a 350° oven. Before removing from oven prepare a mixture of butter, sugar and cream and pour over hot cake. Place under broiler until lightly browned. Serve plain or with whipped cream. Serves 12.

Mrs. Artia Chambers, *Skiatook, Oklahoma*

INSTANT MOCHA CREAM LOG

1 cup heavy cream
1 cup cold milk
2 teaspoons instant coffee
1 (4½-ounce) package instant

chocolate pudding
1 cup chopped nuts
1 (6-inch) bakery jelly roll

Pour cream and milk into a deep mixing bowl. Add instant coffee and pudding. Beat until well mixed, about 1 minute. Fold in nuts. Gently unroll jelly roll and spread with half of pudding mixture. Roll up and frost with remaining pudding mixture. Freeze until firm. Slice into 6 servings.

Mrs. Olga Jason, *New Bedford, Massachusetts*

ELEGANT MAI TAI MOUSSE

18 ladyfingers, split
2 envelopes unflavored gelatin
½ cup pineapple juice
   (from crushed drained pineapple)
5 egg yolks
¾ cup sugar
¼ teaspoon salt
1 cup milk, scalded
1/3 cup lime juice

1/3 cup white rum
1 (#211) can crushed pineapple,
   well drained
5 egg whites
½ cup sugar
1 cup heavy cream, whipped
¼ cup chopped macadamia nuts
   or walnuts

Line sides and bottom of 9-inch spring pan with split ladyfingers. Soften gelatin in pineapple juice. Beat egg yolks in top of double boiler. Stir in sugar and salt. Blend in milk, cook over boiling water, stirring for 5 minutes or until thickened. Blend in gelatin-pineapple mixture, lime juice and rum. Add well-drained pineapple. Chill until thickened but not set. Beat egg whites, adding sugar. Fold pineapple custard and whipped cream into egg whites. Pour into lined pan. Chill several hours or overnight. To serve, remove pan rim. Sprinkle with nuts. Serves 12.

ORANGE BABA DESSERT

1 (13¾-ounce) package hot roll mix
¾ cup warm water
2 eggs
2 tablespoons melted butter

2 tablespoons sugar
1½ teaspoons grated orange rind
1 tablespoon brandy (or
   2 teaspoons vanilla)

In large mixing bowl, combine warm water with yeast (from hot roll mix). Stir until dissolved. Stir in eggs, melted butter, sugar, orange rind, and brandy. Add flour a little at a time and beat well, until batter resembles cake batter. Butter a 9-inch torte pan; half fill, spooning into pan. Cover and let rise until double in size (about 30 to 45 minutes). Preheat oven to 375°. Bake 20 to 30 minutes, or until brown. (If browning too fast, cover with brown paper.) Turn baba out on a serving dish and baste with hot syrup until all syrup is absorbed. Garnish with sliced almonds. Serves 6.

Orange Baba Syrup

Bring to a boil 1 cup sugar and 1 cup water. Add 1 tablespoon butter and one 6-ounce can frozen orange juice concentrate.

Mrs. Joe Hrvatin, *Spokane, Washington*

INTERNATIONAL SPECIALTIES

The World in Your Hand

BALLOTINE DE DINDE
By Ruth M. Malone

One of the world's experts on bringing exciting new ideas to family dining is Ruth M. Malone, author of The Dogpatch Cook Book, Where to Eat in the Ozarks, *the* Holiday Inn International Cook Book, *and articles beyond mention for national magazines, among them* The Saturday Evening Post. *It is from her recipes in the* Post, *specializing in international flavor, that the following are selected. The peripatetic lady really knows whereof she speaks, worldwide.*

10- to 12-pound turkey
3 black truffles
　(1 small can)
½ cup shelled and
　skinned pistachio
　nuts
6-ounce piece of
　cooked ham
6-ounce piece of
　cooked smoked
　tongue
1 cup dry port
　wine or cognac
Pepper and salt
½ pound butter

¾ pound veal and ¾
　pound pork ground
　together very finely
3 eggs
2 onions, chopped
1 clove garlic
2 teaspoons salt
Dash of pepper
Pinch of allspice
½ teaspoon ground
　thyme
Needle, white
　thread
Butcher's twine

The day before: put out all your ingredients. Dice the truffles, shell pistachio nuts, cut ham and tongue into finger-shaped pieces. Put pork and veal mixture into a large mixing bowl. Add lightly beaten eggs, thyme, allspice, salt, pepper, crushed clove of garlic, ¾ cup of port or cognac. Mix till light. Gently saute the onion in a quarter pound of butter. Take almost 10 minutes to do this, cooking onions so gently that they only yellow and do not brown. Add onions and butter to the bowl. Mix thoroughly. This is the stuffing. Put boned turkey flat on the table, skin side down. Season the meat side (inside) with pepper and remaining wine. Spread a layer of stuffing inside the turkey. Then sprinkle pistachio nuts, truffles, ham and tongue over it. Repeat both steps twice. Sew up turkey. Tie in 4 places as you would a rolled roast, making sure stuffing does not go to the ends. Salt, pepper and brush the skin with melted butter. Store in refrigerator until four hours before dinner. Christmas Day: Roast turkey breast side up in a 350-degree oven, allowing 20 minutes per pound. Keep basting top and sides to insure even browning. Serve with natural pan gravy. Serves 8 to 10 easily. If you wish to serve a wine with the dinner, Chassagne Montrachet 1959 is recommended. It is a mildly sweet white wine that will suit most palates.
(Note: The pate maison used for stuffing the ballotine makes a delicious stuffing for a turkey that has all its bones.)

MERINGUE GLACEE

A memorable dessert that is light enough to follow a Christmas dinner is suggested. You may also use peach ice cream and peach slices, or other combinations.

1 cup sifted
  granulated sugar
4 egg whites
Pinch of salt
¼ teaspoon cream
  of tartar

almond extract
1 quart strawberries
1 quart ice cream
1 cup red
  currant jelly
2 tablespoons cognac

Cover cookie sheet with greased, unglazed brown paper. Beat egg whites until foamy. Add salt, and cream of tartar and continue beating until peaks form. Add sugar very slowly, beating until sugar is dissolved. Add the vanilla. Drop by mounded teaspoonful onto brown paper. Bake in 250-degree oven for 1½ hours. At the end of the time, turn off oven, open door and allow meringues to cool in the oven. Leave on paper until ready to use. Christmas Day: Hull the strawberries. Melt the currant jelly and cognac over a low fire. Put ice cream on the dish, surround it with strawberries. Pour warm sauce on the berries and top with meringues.

RED SNAPPER A LA VERACRUZANA
(Huachinango a la Veracruzana)

1 2½-pound red snapper
2½ cups chopped tomatoes
2 onions, chopped
3 green peppers, chopped
3 cloves garlic, crushed
1 bunch parsley,
  chopped fine
2 chili peppers,
  chopped fine
  (small elongated
  green chili)

1/3 cup finely chopped
  green olives
1/3 cup capers
4 tablespoons vinegar
8 jalapeño peppers
  (cut in half,
  fried and cut in strips)
1 pint oil
1 teaspoon oregano
Salt and pepper
¼ pint dry sherry

Cut red snapper into 6-ounce fillets. Saute the tomatoes in a skillet, adding onions, then green peppers, garlic, parsley and chili peppers. Then add chopped olives, capers, vinegar and jalapeño strips. Blend in oil. Season with oregano, salt and pepper. Simmer slowly until all is tender and thickened. Add sherry during last part of cooking.

In a separate skillet, heat a little oil and add well-washed red snapper fillets. Cover fish with sauce. Cover and cook over low heat 20 minutes. Keep fish from sticking with wide spatula. Serve with rice. Serves 4 to 6.

AUNT ELIZA'S BID FOR FAME
By Sophie Kerr

In my Scotch-Irish family there was one aunt who married among the Pennsylvania Dutch, and it was she who, ever-blessed, imparted the recipe for making the local form of peach pie. It is as follows: Line a pie pan with the raw crust and fill it with halves of very ripe yellow peaches, hollow side up. Lay the peaches close together, sprinkle heavily with granulated sugar, then pour in enough thick sour cream to cover the peach halves, and sprinkle on more sugar if needed. Then put on your crisscross strips, pinch them well at the edges, and slide this concoction into the oven for a slow, careful baking. If you want to add two or three kernels taken from cracked peach stones, you'll have a subtle bitter-almond flavor—indeed, a few peach kernels add chic to any peach pie, whether made a la Aunt Aliza or not.

IRELAND'S GIFT TO APPETITES
By George Rector

If it's a short-term trip, you can get the ingredients ready before you start, and pack them in a large pot and two saucepans. You'll want to scrape six medium-sized carrots, peel four potatoes, dice two green peppers into inch cubes, cut up half a cup of leeks and half a cup of celery crosswise, lay in a dozen small white onions and a cup of canned tomato pulp. Also you pack along a mixture of of a teaspoon of mixed mustard, and a tablespoon each of Worcestershire sauce, A-1 sauce and tomato ketchup. That begins to sound good already to me. Also—this is the business end—three pounds chuck of lamb, a pound of breast of lamb and a pound chuck of beef, all cut into two-inch cubes and with as much fat as possible trimmed off the lamb. It sounds like food for a regiment, I know, but don't try to get more than six grown people into one stew if you serve it outdoors after waiting for it to cook.

Simmer your beef for an hour. Then start the lamb in a separate pan and simmer both for another half hour, skimming the fat off the lamb water all the time. Then lamb and beef go into the big pot, along with the liquid, plus the potatoes and carrots quartered, the green peppers, the onions, leeks and celery. Let them all coop up harmoniously for half an hour. Ten minutes before that, put in the tomato pulp and the seasoning, and take the pot off the fire—but keep it right next door, so she'll stay plenty hot. At Dinty Moore's they garnish the end product with a sprinkling of peas and a tablespoon of chopped parsley, but it's a roaring, ranting fine dish without that extra wrinkle and well worth the two hours of nursing it calls for. Let the rest of the party go off and chase butterflies or listen to the echo; you stick around and startle your and their palates with this stew of stews.

"Eat a little something," that familiar, age-old Jewish welcome, is an almost unnecessary invitation. In the presence of good Jewish cooking, it is nearly impossible to stop eating. *"And it isn't just the food itself,"* explains one young matron. *"It's partly the mood and the memories. I remember that as a child in our New York neighborhood, with the aromas of gefilte fish, roast chicken and yeast cake coming from every house, I couldn't get home fast enough. It was the same every Friday. And the baking of* challah, *that wonderful Sabbath bread, has as much religious fervor as cooking skill. Even now such smells seem to me like Peace and Love and Warmth. You know what I mean. If Betty Crocker could put those smells up in box mixes, we could end juvenile delinquency."*

Jewish cooking today is an amalgam of contributions, picked up by generations of merchants and migrants who wandered the countries of the earth. In the melting-pot processes of the big city these culinary contributions have simmered down to a tasty heritage known as "New York-style Jewish cooking." In the more than three centuries since the first Jewish pioneer group arrived in New Amsterdam, this influence has spread till most cities in the United States today can enjoy its specialties.

GEFILTE FISH

3 pounds carp
2 pounds whitefish
1 pound yellow pike
3 onions
Salt, whole peppercorns

2 eggs
¼ cup water
Salt, white pepper
1 tablespoon cracker meal
2 carrots, scraped

Have fish dealer fillet fish, reserving heads and bones for stock. Salt fillets and refrigerate. Cover heads, bones, two peeled onions, salt and peppercorns with 1 quart water; bring to boil, simmer 20 minutes. Meanwhile put fish fillets and 1 onion through grinder with fine blade. Place in wooden chopping bowl. Add eggs, lightly beaten with water, salt, pepper and cracker meal. Chop mixture till light and well blended. Moisten hands with cold water and shape into loose balls. Slip into boiling stock with a spoon, add water if necessary to cover and simmer 1½ hours. Add carrots and cook another half hour until fish balls are white and about twice original size. Lift fish balls out with slotted spoon. Remove carrots, slice and set aside. Strain stock and pour half over fish. Pour remainder into jar; refrigerate to set. Serve cold, garnishing the fish with sliced carrot and chilled stock. Serves about 12.

SWEET AND SOUR POT ROAST

6 pounds beef
2 large onions, sliced
1 clove minced garlic
¾ cup of water or stock
2 bay leaves
2 tablespoons lemon juice

or vinegar
1 tablespoon brown
  sugar
3 tablespoons ketchup
½ cup raisins
Salt

Brown meat in hot fat on all sides, using heavy pot. Add onions and garlic, cook till brown. Add water or stock and bay leaves; cover and simmer one hour. Add lemon juice and brown sugar. Cover and simmer another hour. Add ketchup, raisins and salt. Cover and cook ½ hour. Serve hot with potato pancakes, noodles or brown rice. Serves 6 to 8 persons.

NOODLE FRUIT CAPON STUFFING

½ pound broad noodles, cooked
4 tablespoons fat (preferably
  chicken fat)
1 medium onion, minced
Liver and gizzards, chopped
1 tablespoon salt
1 teaspoon paprika

¼ teaspoon pepper
¼ teaspoon ginger
2 tablespoons minced parsley
1 cup minced apples
1 cup prunes, stewed and cut
Grated rind of 1 orange
1 beaten egg

Cook noodles, drain, rinse with cold water and drain well. Toss with one tablespoon of fat. Heat remaining fat, add onions, liver, gizzards, seasonings and parsley; brown. Stir in apples, prunes and grated rind. Add mixture to noodles in a large bowl, toss. Stir in beaten egg. Pack stuffing loosely in cavity of 6- to 8-pound capon, truss. Rub outside of capon with oil, place breast up in shallow roasting pan and bake in 350° oven for two to two and a half hours, basting with oil from time to time.

SABBATH CHOLENT

3 to 4 pounds of beef
1 pound dried Lima beans
3 large onions, sliced
¼ cup chicken fat
Salt, pepper and paprika

1 small clove garlic
½ pound barley
2 tablespoons flour
Boiling water to cover

For the meat use flanken or brisket. Soak beans overnight; then drain. Using heavy-duty pot, brown onions in hot fat, remove. Rub meat generously with salt, pepper, paprika, and garlic. Brown well in hot fat. Add all ingredients; sprinkle lightly with flour. Add boiling water to cover. Cover tightly and bring to boil. Taste, adjust salt, pepper. To finish cooking, place covered pot in 250° oven overnight and until noon next day or cook in 350˙ oven for 3 to 4 hours. Serves 10 to 12.

RICH NOODLE PUDDING

½ pound medium egg noodles
3 tablespoons butter
1 package (8 ounces) cream
  cheese
½ pound cottage cheese
½ cup sour cream
3 eggs, separated
½ teaspoon salt

½ cup sugar
1 teaspoon cinnamon
1 cup sliced peeled apples
¼ cup broken walnut
  meats
1 teaspoon grated lemon
  rind
½ cup white raisins

Cook noodles in boiling, salted water. Drain. Toss with butter in large bowl.
Break up cream cheese with fork, add cottage cheese and sour cream and
beat until light. Add egg yolks, beat well. Pour over noodles in bowl. Add
remaining ingredients, except egg whites, and mix well. Beat egg whites stiff,
fold in. Pour into greased casserole. Bake in 350° oven about 45 minutes, or
until browned. Serves 6.

DANISH-AMERICAN WINNER
By Robert W. Wells

Mrs. Beck's Honskekod suppe *(chicken soup) with meat balls and dumplings:*

Soup:

One 3- to 4-pound chicken
2 teaspoons salt
1 soup wisp (celery leaves and

parsley tied together)
1 small onion
2 or 3 small whole carrots

Meatballs:

1 pound ground pork
1 cup milk
1 medium-sized onion
½ teaspoon pepper

1/3 cup flour (or bread
  crumbs)
1 egg
1 teaspoon salt

Dumplings:

1 cup boiling water
½ cup butter
1 cup flour

4 eggs
½ teaspoon salt

Cut up chicken. Place in boiling water. Add wisp, onion, carrots, salt.
Water should just cover chicken. Simmer until done.

To make meatballs, stir milk into ground pork, adding grated onion, flour
or bread crumbs, egg, salt, pepper. Mix thoroughly. Form into balls. Boil
until done in salt water.

Dumplings: Melt butter in boiling water. Add flour and beat until smooth.
Cool, then add eggs, one at a time, and beat well. Add salt. Use teaspoon to
drop dumpling mix into hot but not boiling salt water. Bring to boil,
agitating water gently so dumplings will turn over. Boil about two minutes.

Put several dumplings and meat balls into each dish. Slice carrots and put
a few slices into each dish. Remove chicken from soup and serve it separately. Remove wisp, which may be thrown away or eaten by the cook. Pour
soup on top of dumplings and meatballs. Garnish with sprinkled parsley.
Serves 6 to 8.

VONDERFUL NICE
By Bill Wolf

Picnics bring out the cat in Dutch women. They contrive to sample rival cooks' products, conceal their own recipes and try to acquire those of other women. A confirmed taster will try everything on the long tables, then say to a select group of friends: "That potato salad made by Sadie Habecker, it's vonderful nice, of course, but"—she will pause judiciously—"it don't seem to have zaktly the right amount of bacon drippin's. Do you spose she uses celery salt as vell as celery?"

Everything really did taste "vonderful nice"—Dutch cold pressed chicken, cold ham, beef, pork, cold fried chicken, pickled and deviled eggs, an amazing variety of cakes and pies, and always the Dutch potato salad. There are many variations. This is the way I know it best:

Boil and cube eight potatoes or cut them in thick half slices. Add diced celery, four chopped hard-boiled eggs, at least one onion chopped fine—even more skilled cooks scrape the juice from the onion over the potatoes. Now for the dressing: Fry eight slices of bacon cut into small pieces. In a separate bowl, mix a half cup of water, same amount of vinegar, a half teaspoon of salt, quarter teaspoon each of dry mustard and black pepper, two well-beaten eggs. Stir and add to hot bacon and fat.

After this mixture thickened on the stove, it was poured over the cold ingredients, everything was stirred slightly and set aside to cool. A somewhat similar sour dressing, minus the mustard and plus some butter, cream and sugar, is poured hot over dandelions in the spring for greens, or on lettuce leaves.

SHOOFLY PIE

Then there are the pies, such as the famous shoofly, which are really cakes in a pastry shell. Addicts of the shoofly—the name is probably a corruption of chouflour, since the finished pie somewhat resembles a cauliflower—are sharply divided into Wets and Drys, although both camps would probably agree that the molasses that goes into a shoofly is the most important factor. With many perfectionist cooks, the bottled variety will not do; real barrel molasses is a necessity. In any case, ¾ cup of baking molasses is mixed with a well-beaten egg yolk and ¾ cup of boiling water in which 2 teaspoons of baking soda have been dissolved. In another bowl, ¾ cup of flour is sifted with ½ cup of brown sugar; 1/8 teaspoon each of nutmeg, ginger and cloves; ½ teaspoon of cinnamon and ¼ teaspoon of salt, and worked into 2 table-spoons of shortening to form crumbs. A pie dish is lined with pastry, and alternate layers of the liquid and the crumb mixture are added, topping with the latter. It is baked at 450 degrees until the edges are brown, then the oven is reduced to 350 degrees, and the shoofly is baked until firm. For a "wetter" shoofly—one with a stickier bottom—more molasses is added.

Also characteristically Pennsylvania Dutch are milk pies. As the name implies, milk or buttermilk is poured into a crust, a bit of sugar and butter are added with 2 teaspoonfuls of flour and a dash of cinnamon and nutmeg, and the whole baked in a hot oven. All laws of cookery would indicate that the only result would be an inedible mess and an oven in need of immediate cleaning, but strangely enough a delicate custard emerges.

KUGEL
(Potato Casserole)

10 medium potatoes
1 small onion
1 teaspoon salt

Generous amount of garlic powder
¼ cup flour
2 tablespoons chicken fat

Chop potatoes and onions in blender. (Do one or two potatoes at a time, adding a little water each time. Then strain all.) Add all remaining ingredients: place in casserole and dot mixture with chicken fat. Bake, uncovered, for 1 hour at 400°. Cover casserole and bake a second hour at 350°. Serves 6.

Jennifer Gould, *Brighton, Massachusetts*

CHICKEN AND PORK MECHADA
(Philippine)

1 young chicken
  cut into regular pieces
1 pound lean pork, cubed
1 onion, diced
½ cup shortening
Salt and pepper
1 (15½-ounce) can tomato sauce

1 (8-ounce) can tomato paste
3 potatoes, quartered
3 carrots, quartered
½ red pepper, sliced
½ green pepper, sliced
1 can sweet peas
Rice

Sauté chicken, pork and onions in shortening in 6-quart Dutch oven. Season with salt and pepper. Add tomato sauce and tomato paste. Simmer for 10 minutes. Add potatoes, carrots and red and green peppers, and cook for 30 minutes or until meat is tender. Add sweet peas and simmer another 5 minutes. Serve with boiled rice, if desired. Serves 6.

Remy J. Garcia, *Peru, Indiana*

CAMARON REBOSADO
(Philippine Fried Shrimp)

1 pound shrimp
1 tablespoon salt
2 eggs
3 tablespoons flour

1 tablespoon cornstarch
1 teaspoon baking powder
Fat for frying

Sprinkle shrimp with salt and let stand for 1 hour. Beat eggs; add flour, cornstarch and baking powder. Mix thoroughly. Dip shrimp one at a time into batter and fry in deep fat.

Carmen Wilhelm, *Centreville, Virginia*

AUTHENTIC SPANISH BEAN SOUP

¾ pound garbanzos (chick-peas)
1 teaspoon salt
  (for soaking garbanzos)
1 beef bone
1 ham bone
1½ quarts water

4 ounces whole bacon
1 onion
½ pound potatoes
1 pinch saffron
1 tablespoon salt
1 chorizo (Spanish sausage)

Soak garbanzos overnight with one teaspoon salt in water to cover. Before cooking, drain salted water and put garbanzos, beef bone and ham bone in 1½ quarts water. Cook 45 minutes over slow fire. Fry bacon and finely chopped onion. Place in pan, adding potatoes, saffron and salt. When potatoes are almost done, add chorizo cut in thin slices. Simmer 20 to 25 minutes. Serves 6.

Shirley Martin, *Tampa, Florida*

LATVIAN MIDSUMMER CHEESE

½ gallon fresh milk
5 pounds dry cottage cheese
1 stick butter or margarine

4 eggs
1 teaspoon salt
2 tablespoons caraway seeds

In a large kettle pour milk. Add dry cottage cheese and stir until it begins to boil. Turn off heat. Place cheesecloth in a large bowl. Add the boiled mixture. Take the corners of the cheesecloth to the top, let the liquid drip out, then squeeze cheesecloth as dry as possible. Place dry cheese in a bowl with the butter or margarine, eggs, salt and caraway seeds. With wooden spoon stir until it is well mixed and the cheese is solid in one piece.

Irma Henkels, *Indianapolis, Indiana*

SERINA KAKER
(Norwegian Cookie)

1¾ sticks butter or margarine
1 1/8 cups sugar
2 eggs, separated
2¼ cups flour, sifted

1½ teaspoons baking powder
1 teaspoon vanilla
50 almonds, chopped

Cream butter and sugar. Add 2 egg yolks and one egg white and mix well. Sift flour and baking powder together and add to batter. Add vanilla and form small round balls about one inch in diameter. Place on lightly greased cookie sheet and press down with bottom of glass. Brush with other egg white and sprinkle with almonds. Bake in 350° oven until very light golden. Do not let brown. Yield: 4 dozen.

Mrs. William Wesely, *Wayne, New Jersey*

HUNGARIAN KALACS

2 fresh yeast cakes
1 cup lukewarm water
4 tablespoons sugar
½ cup butter, melted

4½ cups flour
2 egg yolks
1 teaspoon salt

Filling:

½ cup milk
1½ pounds ground walnuts
½ cup sugar

1 tablespoon butter
1 teaspoon lemon juice

Crumble yeast and add water and sugar. Let stand 5 minutes. Mix melted butter and flour as for pie crust. Make a well and add egg yolks, salt and yeast mixture. Stir until smooth and dough leaves sides of bowl. Divide into 4 pieces and roll out as thin as possible; spread with filling. Place on greased pan and brush with egg white, very gently. Let stand in warm place for 1 hour. Bake at 350° for 30 minutes or until light brown. Cover with damp cloth as soon as it comes from the oven. Keep covered about 10 minutes to make a nice crust.

Directions for filling: Heat milk; add walnuts and stir. Add sugar, butter and lemon juice. Cool before spreading on dough.

Helen Horvath, *Fort Lauderdale, Florida*

"I'm afraid that's going to break the spell."